ENDORSEMENTS

"For two decades (or longer), evangelicals have been making a steady retreat from practically every front of historic contention with the doctrines of the Roman Catholic Church. The statement called Evangelicals & Catholics Together accelerated the quest for evangelical-Catholic détente in the mid-1990s. Many evangelicals seem to think this is a positive, unifying movement. I'm convinced it is a dangerous drift. From the time I began to detect this new ecumenical climate until now, one the few voices sounding a clear and consistent warning about it has always been R. C. Sproul's. He sees clearly that what is at stake is nothing less than the gospel. The various recent ecumenical manifestoes all demonstrate this, albeit in subtle, confusing terms. More proof is found in the published teachings of the Roman Catholic Church herself. For at least fifteen years, I have wished for a clear, accessible exposé using the most recent Roman Catholic catechism to show why that church's doctrine is incompatible with—even hostile to—the true gospel of Jesus Christ. I'm especially glad now to have just such a book from the pen of Dr. Sproul. No one is better qualified than he to speak definitively to the issues, and he has done a superb job of making the case from Scripture, from church history, and from the Catechism of the Catholic Church itself."

—Dr. John MacArthur
Pastor-teacher, Grace Community Church
Sun Valley, Calif.

"We live at a time when evangelicalism's theological chaos and preference for parachurch pyrotechnics over biblical ecclesiology have made Rome an increasingly attractive option for many Christians seeking something more intellectually and institutionally satisfying. This is why Dr. Sproul's book is so timely, as it sets out the differences between orthodox Protestantism and Roman Catholicism in a clear, concise, and helpful way. Anyone wanting to know what is at stake in the debate between Geneva and Rome should read this book."

—Dr. Carl R. Trueman
Paul Woolley Chair of Church History
Westminster Theological Seminary, Philadelphia

"When discussing Roman Catholic theology, Protestants have too often been ignorant, careless, or unfair. The power of this book is that R. C. Sproul is fair, precise, and charitable as he proves that the errors of the Roman Catholic Church are both deep and significant, and that the Roman Catholic gospel is not the gospel of the Bible. Even as he calls for us to love our Roman Catholic friends, he warns that we cannot consider them brothers and sisters when the gospel itself is at stake."

—TIM CHALLIES
Pastor, Grace Fellowship Church, Toronto
Blogger, www.challies.com

"Some are drawn to Roman Catholicism because of the rich tradition they see in it but do not see in much of evangelicalism. Even church leaders and historians are telling us the Protestant/Roman Catholic divide is over. We need a biblically sound and historically informed answer. This book is the answer. With his characteristic persuasion and clarity, R. C. Sproul shows the errors of Roman Catholicism when viewed against the beauty and truth of the gospel of Jesus Christ revealed in Scripture."

—DR. STEPHEN J. NICHOLS
President
Reformation Bible College, Sanford, Fla.

"Truth is precious, for it sets us free (John 8:31–32). In Christ's church, our unity revolves around knowing what we believe (Eph. 4:12–13). Too often discussions about Roman Catholicism and Protestantism are marred by indifference to doctrine or unfair caricatures of each other's beliefs. In neither case do we love the truth. R. C. Sproul's book is a masterpiece of fairness, brimming with quotations from authoritative Catholic and Protestant writings. In a short scope he gives us a clear view of the central questions of the Reformation. He helps us to see that we cannot minimize our differences and remain faithful to Christ, for the gospel itself is at stake."

—DR. JOEL R. BEEKE
President and professor of systematic theology and homiletics
Puritan Reformed Theological Seminary, Grand Rapids, Mich.

"This is a terrific book, one I have been hoping to find for a long time. Sproul firmly and rightly defends the faith of the Reformation, but without resorting to rancor or caricature. He takes great pains to be fair to Rome, considering the nuances of the Catholic Catechism and the significance of Vatican II. This will be the first book I recommend when either Protestants or Catholics ask me what is the difference between the two."

—REV. KEVIN DEYOUNG
Senior pastor, University Reformed Church
East Lansing, Mich.

"An enormously important book at a turning point in relationships between Roman Catholics and Protestants. It displays everything we would expect from Dr. Sproul: clarity, precision, honesty, and deeply held conviction about the nature and substance of a continuing disagreement. Crucial reading written with courage and grace."

—DR. DEREK W. H. THOMAS
Senior Minister
First Presbyterian Church, Columbia, S.C.

"This book is not what you might assume: a rehearsal of slogans. Rather, it is an intelligent and engaging primer for Protestants and Roman Catholics alike about what Rome actually teaches and what are the profound issues that continue to separate confessional, evangelical Protestants from the Roman communion. This is a book that Protestants should give to their Roman Catholic neighbors and that Protestant pastors (after reading it) should give to their members. It is also a book that more than a few theologians and historians should read before the next round of ecumenical discussions and documents."

—DR. R. SCOTT CLARK
Professor of church history and historical theology
Westminster Seminary California, Escondido, Calif.

"In this irenic, though uncompromising, response to recent attempts by evangelicals to say that nothing substantial in terms of key doctrines now divides them from contemporary Roman Catholicism, R. C. Sproul rightly shows that this is deeply misguided thinking. On core issues that relate to the nature of salvation and the church, Sproul ever so carefully and judiciously spells out the way that Roman Catholic thought is as far away as it has ever been from that of the Reformers, and that, if we are to be true to the Scriptures, we cannot move beyond the lines established at the time of the Reformation. What is at stake is nothing less than the nature of the gospel. This is an extremely helpful book that should be required reading for all interested in relating to Roman Catholics today."

—DR. MICHAEL A. G. HAYKIN
Professor of church history and biblical spirituality
The Southern Baptist Theological Seminary, Louisville, Ky.

"We will soon be observing the five-hundredth anniversary of the Protestant Reformation. At a time when some are questioning the relevance and importance of the Reformation to the evangelical church, R. C. Sproul's survey of the leading differences between Protestantism and Roman Catholicism is both welcome and needed. Liberally referencing and explaining the official teaching of the Roman Catholic Church, Sproul carefully shows what are—and are not—the differences between Rome and Protestantism. Writing in the way that we have come to expect—clearly, accessibly, and pastorally—Sproul convincingly demonstrates that the issues that stirred the Reformers centuries ago not only strike at the heart of the gospel but also remain with us today. In a day when many evangelicals are giving renewed attention to the biblical gospel, Sproul's work admirably assists the church in articulating the gospel faithfully and wisely."

—DR. GUY PRENTISS WATERS
James M. Baird Jr. Professor of New Testament
Reformed Theological Seminary, Jackson, Miss.

ARE WE TOGETHER?

*A Protestant Analyzes
Roman Catholicism*

R.C. SPROUL

IR *Reformation Trust*   A DIVISION OF LIGONIER MINISTRIES, ORLANDO, FL

Are We Together? A Protestant Analyzes Roman Catholicism

© 2012 by R.C. Sproul

Published by Reformation Trust Publishing
a division of Ligonier Ministries
421 Ligonier Court, Sanford, FL 32771
Ligonier.org   ReformationTrust.com

Printed in Crawforsville, IN
RR Donnelley & Sons.
February 2016
First edition, second printing

Cover design: Dual Identity
Interior design and typeset: Katherine Lloyd, The DESK

Library of Congress Cataloging-in-Publication Data

Sproul, R. C. (Robert Charles), 1939-
    Are we together? : a Protestant analyzes Roman Catholicism / R.C. Sproul. -- 1st ed.
        p. cm.
    Includes bibliographical references and index.
    ISBN 978-1-56769-282-2
    1. Reformed Church--Relations--Catholic Church. 2. Catholic Church--Relations--Reformed Church. 3. Protestant churches--Relations--Catholic Church. 4. Catholic Church--Relations--Protestant churches. 5. Catholic Church--Doctrines. 6. Reformed Church--Doctrines. 7. Protestant churches--Doctrines. I. Title.
    BX9419.5.C38S67 2012
    280'.042--dc23   2012018240

To R. C. Sproul Jr.,
in memory of his wife,
Denise Sproul

CONTENTS

COMBATING THE DRIFT

Even among evangelical Protestants, there is a widespread assumption that the Reformation is over. We hear it said that the questions that divided Western Christendom in the sixteenth century are remote from the problems of contemporary life. Besides, the argument continues, ecumenical rapprochements have defused the mutual condemnations. The Roman Catholic Magisterium now affirms a robust doctrine of grace in salvation and the churches of the Reformation finally have come to acknowledge the role of human agency. In the face of aggressive secularism and a culture of death, not to mention a resurgent Islamic movement across the globe, are not our divisions—and the polemics that sustain them—both unnecessary and a scandal to our common witness?

Widely recognized as a leading Christian professor, pastor, writer, and teacher, R. C. Sproul disagrees with this assumption. An avid student of Thomas Aquinas, he belongs to a long tradition of Reformed theologians who have read widely and profitably in the pre-Reformation heritage. Like the Reformers, he knows that the medieval church always affirmed—and official Roman Catholic teaching today affirms—the importance of grace, Christ, faith, and Scripture. It was the *sola* (Latin: "alone") that the Reformers attached to these affirmations that provoked the Reformation and continues to divide these historical bodies. Sproul knows where these confessions agree on substantial matters and where they diverge in equally significant ways. This knowledge makes this book a learned exploration that avoids sweeping caricatures, as well as sweeping announcements that we have finally resolved our differences.

Through the years, many Protestants themselves have drifted from the core convictions that ignited the Reformation. Whole denominations with Reformation roots have wandered so far from God's Word toward a human-centered philosophy and spirituality that our differences with Rome seem slight by comparison. While the Reformers discerned in the medieval church a creeping Semi-Pelagianism that is natural to the fallen heart, many Protestant bodies today entertain and even encourage an outright Pelagianism. If our condition is not as grave as Scripture indicates, it is not surprising that our perception of salvation shifts from a rescue operation by God incarnate to our own personal and social progress and transformation. Jesus becomes an inspiring example, of course, but He hardly needs to be a divine Savior to fulfill this role. Not surprisingly, the divinization of the inner self (Gnosticism) and a denial of Christ's unique person and work (Arianism/Socinianism) ensue, as night follows day. No one needs to announce this fact. No formal break with Christianity is necessary. The creeds may still be affirmed, but they no longer matter, because our faith and life are determined more by our natural theology than by the surprising and disorienting gospel.

This drift, away from the light of God's Word and back to the orbit of our fallen hearts, is as evident today in evangelical circles where Reformation essentials were defended and proclaimed with passion. According to several studies, American evangelicals generally do not know what they believe and why they believe it.

Consequently, most share with the wider culture a confidence in human goodness and a weak view of the need for God's saving grace in Jesus Christ. According to these reports, most evangelicals believe that we are saved by being good and that there are many ways of salvation apart from explicit faith in Jesus Christ.

So, if the question of the Reformation—"How can I find a gracious God?"—is no longer relevant, then Christianity is no longer relevant. And if evangelical Protestantism has lost its frame of reference for answering that question, it makes sense that the doctrinal divisions of the Reformation seem irrelevant when there is so much for us to do together in order to transform our world.

For the author of this book, though, the Reformation, far from being over, needs to sweep across the landscape of contemporary church life—Protestant as well as Roman Catholic. Here are a few of the disturbing trends that need to be checked and reformed:

• We are all too confident in our own words, so that churches become echo chambers for the latest trends in pop psychology, marketing, politics, entertainment, and entrepreneurial leadership. We need to recover our confidence in the triune God and His speech, as He addresses us authoritatively in His Word.

• We are all too confident in our own methods for success in personal, ecclesial, and social transformation. We need to be turned again to God's judgment and grace, His action through His ordained means of grace.

• We are all too confident in our own good works. We need to repent and be brought again to despair not only of our sins but of our pretended righteousness.

• We are all too enamored of our own glory, the kingdoms that we are building. We need to be brought back to that place of trust in Christ where we are deeply aware of "receiving a kingdom that cannot be shaken" (Heb. 12:28), because God is building it for His own glory, and the gates of hell cannot prevail against it. Only as we turn our ears away from the false promises of this passing age to God's Word, to His saving revelation in Christ as the only gospel, and to the glory of the triune God as our only goal, can we expect to see a genuine revival of Christian discipleship, worship, and mission in the world today.

Even if you do not agree with everything in this book, you will find here the counsel of a wise, faithful, and well-informed pastor. Sproul is passionate about defending the Reformation not as a curator of a museum but as a shepherd of Christ's flock. It is precisely because these questions remain the enduring and ineradicable issue for every human being in every place since the fall of humanity in Eden that he persistently draws our attention back to them. I have been shaped, provoked, and instructed by his laser-like focus on these questions throughout my adult life.

May the Spirit of God illumine our minds and hearts to hear and understand His Word along the important and sometimes difficult path that the author blazes in these pages. Through it, may we be not only clearer in understanding where we differ from our Roman Catholic friends, but more delighted in the treasure laid up for us in God's living and abiding Word.

—Dr. Michael S. Horton
Professor of systematic theology and apologetics
Westminster Seminary California

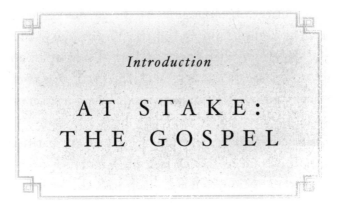

AT STAKE:
THE GOSPEL

THE GOSPEL OF JESUS CHRIST is always at risk of distortion. It became distorted in the centuries leading up to the Protestant Reformation of the sixteenth century. It became distorted at innumerable other points of church history, and it is often distorted today. This is why Martin Luther said the gospel must be defended in every generation. It is the center point of attack by the forces of evil. They know that if they can get rid of the gospel, they can get rid of Christianity.

There are two sides to the gospel, the good news of the New Testament: an objective side and a subjective side. The objective content of the gospel is the person and work of Jesus—who He is and what He accomplished in His life. The subjective side is the question of how the benefits of Christ's work are appropriated to the believer. There the doctrine of justification comes to the fore.

Many issues were involved in the Reformation, but the core matter, the material issue of the Reformation, was the gospel, especially the doctrine of justification. There was no great disagreement between the Roman Catholic Church authorities and the Protestant

Reformers about the objective side. All the parties agreed that Jesus was divine, the Son of God and of the Virgin Mary, and that He lived a life of perfect obedience, died on the cross in an atoning death, and was raised from the grave. The battle was over the second part of the gospel, the subjective side, the question of how the benefits of Christ are applied to the believer.

The Reformers believed and taught that we are justified by faith alone. Faith, they said, is the *sole instrumental cause* for our justification. By this they meant that we receive all the benefits of Jesus' work through putting our trust in Him alone.

The Roman communion also taught that faith is a necessary condition for salvation. At the seminal Council of Trent (1545–1563), which formulated Rome's response to the Reformation, the Roman Catholic authorities declared that faith affords three things: the *initium*, the *fundamentum*, and the *radix*. That is, faith is the *beginning* of justification, the *foundation* for justification, and the *root* of justification. But Rome held that a person can have true faith and still not be justified, because there was much more to the Roman system.

In reality, the Roman view of the gospel, as expressed at Trent, was that justification is accomplished through the sacraments. Initially, the recipient must accept and cooperate in baptism, by which he receives justifying grace. He retains that grace until he commits a mortal sin. Mortal sin is called "mortal" because it kills the grace of justification. The sinner then must be justified a second time. That happens through the sacrament of penance, which the Council of Trent defined as "a second plank" of justification for those who have made shipwreck of their souls.[1]

The fundamental difference was this. Trent said that God does not justify anyone until real righteousness inheres within the person. In other words, God does not declare a person righteous unless he or she *is* righteous. So, according to Roman Catholic doctrine, justification depends on a person's sanctification. By contrast, the

Reformers said justification is based on the imputation of the righteousness of Jesus. The only ground by which a person can be saved is Jesus' righteousness, which is reckoned to him when he believes.

There were radically different views of salvation. They could not be reconciled. One of them was the gospel. One of them was not. Thus, what was at stake in the Reformation was the gospel of Jesus Christ. Though the Council of Trent made many fine affirmations of traditional truths of the Christian faith, it declared justification by faith alone to be anathema,[2] ignoring many plain teachings of Scripture, such as Romans 3:28: "For we hold that one is justified by faith apart from works of the law."

Liberalism and ecumenism

In the nineteenth and twentieth centuries, the gospel was threatened by theological liberals who denied the supernatural work of Jesus. This was still the biggest threat when I entered seminary in the 1960s. Eventually the compromises were so blatant I had to leave the church in which I was raised and ordained.

About ten years after I was ordained, a minister of the denomination in which I was ordained was tried in a church court for heresy. Such trials were nearly a thing of the past, but this man had publicly denied the atonement of Christ and would not affirm the deity of Christ as an ordained minister. His case went to the highest court of the church.

When that court handed down its decision, it made two affirmations. First, the court reaffirmed the church's historical creeds, all of which declared the deity of Christ and the atonement of Christ. Then the court went on to say that this man's views were within the limits of interpretation of the creed. So, on the one hand, the court reaffirmed the creeds, but on the other hand, it said ministers in the church did not really have to believe the creeds.

That case showed me that the denomination in which I was

serving was willing to tolerate the intolerable. A man could deny the deity of Christ or the atonement of Christ and remain a minister in good standing. This crisis revealed a deep-rooted and widespread antipathy to objective confessional truth.

I think the biggest crisis over the purity of the gospel that I have experienced in my ministerial career was the initiative known as Evangelicals & Catholics Together (ECT, 1994). This initiative was driven by deep concern among some leading evangelicals and Roman Catholics over so-called "common-grace issues," such as family values, abortion, and relativism in the culture. Protestant and Roman Catholic leaders wanted to join hands to speak as Christians united against this growing tide of moral decay and relativism. All that was fine. I would march with anyone—Roman Catholics, Mormons, even Muslims—for civil rights for people and unborn babies.

But in the middle of the ECT document, the framers said, "We affirm together that we are justified by grace through faith because of Christ."[3] In other words, ECT stated that evangelicals and Roman Catholics have a unity of faith in the gospel. This statement went too far. If I march with a Muslim because we agree on certain human rights, that's one thing. It is another thing to say I have a unity of faith with the Muslim. That is not true at all. Neither is it true that I, as an evangelical, have a unity of faith with Roman Catholics. So, that initial document provoked quite a controversy within evangelicalism.

It was followed by ECT II: The Gift of Salvation (1997), which addressed much more fully the theological concerns that various people had expressed after the first initiative, particularly about justification. The two sides, evangelicals and Roman Catholics, affirmed agreement on many aspects of justification, including the requirement of faith. But in the end, they left the language of imputation on the table. In my judgment, this document was far worse than the first one because the framers were willing to maintain their assertion of the unity of faith in the gospel without affirming impu-tation, which was the core issue in the sixteenth century.

The doctrine of imputation is, for me, the nonnegotiable. In 1541, at the Colloquy of Regensburg, there were serious efforts by the magisterial Reformers to reconcile with Rome. They came close, but ultimately they could not reconcile their competing views on imputation. Luther stressed that the only righteousness believers have in the sight of God is an *alien* righteousness, that is, the righ-teousness of Christ that God imputes, or reckons, to them. They have no hope of becoming so inherently righteous that God will accept them. If I had to become inherently righteous before God would accept me, I would despair of Christianity tomorrow.

In 2009, a new document was released, The Manhattan Decla-ration: A Call of Christian Conscience. It was another effort to find common cause on such issues as the sanctity of life, traditional mar-riage, and religious liberty. The signers included evangelical, Roman Catholic, and Orthodox adherents. It was similar in many respects to the ECT initiative and was driven by many of the same people. Unfortunately, it gave the same blanket endorsement of Rome as a Christian body.

The Manhattan Declaration says, "Christians are heirs of a 2,000-year tradition of proclaiming God's Word." But who are the Christians it is speaking about? The document refers to "Orthodox, Catholic, and Evangelical Christians." Furthermore, it calls Chris-tians to unite in "the Gospel," "the Gospel of costly grace," and "the Gospel of our Lord and Savior Jesus Christ," and it says it is our duty to proclaim this gospel "both in season and out of season."[4] This document confuses the gospel and obscures the distinction between who is and is not a Christian. I do not believe that the Roman Catholic and Orthodox churches are preaching the same gospel that evangelicals preach.

For these reasons, I could not sign the Manhattan Declaration, and neither could such men as John MacArthur, Michael Horton, and Alistair Begg. We were in agreement with ninety-nine percent of what was in the declaration, and we all strenuously support the sanctity of life, traditional marriage, and religious liberty. But we could not agree with the declaration in its ecumenical assertion.

One of the ironies of ECT was that, among other things, the framers wanted to overcome relativism in the culture. However, they ended up relativizing the most important truth of all—the gospel.

Misunderstanding and confusion

I think ECT and similar efforts to make common cause with Roman Catholics are based on a fundamental misunderstanding of where the Roman Catholic Church is theologically and what it actually teaches. There is no question that the Roman Catholic Church has changed since the sixteenth century. But the changes have not closed the gap between Rome and Protestantism. Indeed, the differences are greater now. For instance, the formally defined proclamation of the infallibility of the pope and all of the Mariology statements have come since the Reformation. Neither has Rome backed down from any of the positions it took in the sixteenth-century debate. In the updated Catechism of the Catholic Church, released in the mid-1990s, the treasury of merit, purgatory, indulgences, justification through the sacraments, and other doctrines were reaffirmed.

I think this misunderstanding has been driven primarily by confusion over the significance of Vatican Council II (1962–65). It was only the second ecumenical council of the Roman Catholic Church since Trent, the other being Vatican Council I (1869–70). So, these councils are rare events, and the church and the world were surprised when Pope John XXIII convened Vatican II.

The statements produced by Vatican I referred to Protestants as schismatics and heretics. In marked contrast, the rhetoric of Vatican II was kind, warm, and appeasing. Protestants were called "separated brethren." John's passion, which he set forth in a pastoral letter, was that the Lord's sheepfold would be one. There should be unity under one shepherd, he said, with all Christians returning to Holy Mother Church under the Roman pontiff.[5] John was seen as kind, avuncular, and warm, so people jumped to the conclusion that Rome had changed its theology. However, many overlooked the fact that John ruled out any debate about justification at Vatican II.

In the same era as Vatican II, there was a major split within the Roman Catholic Church between the Western and Latin wings of the church. Much of the Western wing adopted what was called the *nouvelle théologie*, "the new theology," which was much more compatible with historical Protestantism than the classical orthodox Latin Roman theology.

Incidentally, this rupture shows that the contemporary Roman Catholic communion is not as monolithic as it traditionally has been. Some see this rupture as almost as serious as the Reformation. We can find priests and even bishops who sound Protestant in their views. But it is important to remember that when we analyze the Roman Catholic Church, we are not talking about the American church, the Dutch church, the German church, or the Swiss church. We are talking about the *Roman* Catholic Church. The supreme pontiff of the Roman Catholic Church is not the bishop of New York or Los Angeles. He is not the bishop of Berlin, Heidelberg, or Vienna. He is the bishop of *Rome*. He is the one who, along with church councils, defines the belief system of the Roman Catholic Church.

The new theology made great inroads, particularly in Germany, Holland, and the United States. As a result, Roman Catholic priests in these countries began to sound like Protestants in the things they taught. They said they believed in justification by faith alone. Nevertheless, their beliefs did not reflect the church's official positions.

These changes have led many Protestants to join the Roman Catholic Church. I suspect there are vastly greater numbers leaving

Rome for evangelicalism than the other way around, but a number of leading evangelicals have embraced Rome, the most high profile of whom was probably Francis Beckwith, who resigned as president of the Evangelical Theological Society in 2007 when he decided to convert to Roman Catholicism.

I think there are several reasons for these conversions. First, those who are going to Rome love the Roman liturgy, seeing it as more transcendent than the informal and contemporary worship practiced in a growing number of evangelical churches. They long for the beauty, the sense of gravity, and the transcendent majesty of classical worship. I think this is the biggest factor pulling evangelicals toward the Roman Catholic Church.

Second, Protestantism seems to be splintered into an infinite number of divisions and troubled by endless disputes and discussions of doctrine, while Rome seems unified and doctrinally settled. This appeals to many who long for unity, peace, and certainty.

In the midst of all this, a 2005 book actually asked, "Is the Reformation Over?" and asserted "Things are not the way they used to be."[6] My response to this idea that the Reformation is over is that the authors did not understand either the Reformation, Protestantism, Roman Catholicism, or all three. The Reformation was simply a commitment to biblical truth, and as long as there are departures from biblical truth, we have to be involved in the task of reformation. So, when people say the Reformation is over, that we no longer need to fight the battles the Reformers fought and that we can make peace with Rome, they reveal a serious lack of understanding of the historical and current issues that divide Protestants and Roman Catholics.

The indisputable fact is that Rome made a number of strong, clear theological affirmations at the Council of Trent. Because Trent was an ecumenical council, it had all the weight of the infallibility of the church behind it. So, there is a sense in which Rome, in order to maintain her triumphant view of the authority of the church and of tradition, cannot repeal the canons and decrees of the Council of Trent. As recently as the Catechism of the Catholic Church at the end of the twentieth century, it made clear, unambiguous reaffirmations of Trent's teachings. So, those who argue that these teachings on justification are no longer relevant to the debate between Protestantism and Roman Catholicism are simply ignoring what the church itself teaches. Yes, there are some Roman Catholic priests and scholars who dispute some of the teachings of their communion, but as far as the Roman hierarchy is concerned, the Council of Trent stands immutable on its teaching regarding justification. We cannot ignore what Trent said in evaluating where we stand in relation to the Roman Catholic Church and the ongoing relevance of the Reformation.

Thankfully, we are witnessing today an upsurge of interest in the biblical gospel marked by endeavors such as Together for the Gospel, which sponsors conferences that pull together thousands of ministers and laypeople, most of whom are in their twenties and thirties. It is this young group that excites me. We are seeing a new generation of young ministers who are committed to Reformational and biblical truth. My hope is that they will become more and more grounded in the theology they are embracing.

Rome vs. Protestantism

In this book, I have a simple goal. I want to look at Roman Catholic teaching in several significant areas and compare it with Protestant teaching. I hope to show, often using her own words, that the Roman Catholic Church has not changed from what it believed and taught at the time of the Reformation. That means that the Reformation is not over and we must continue to stand firm in proclaiming the biblical gospel.

We begin by looking at the authority of Scripture, which was the formal cause of the Protestant Reformation, then turn to the material cause of the Reformation, the question of justification. Next, we look at the Roman Catholic Church's notion of the relationship of the visible church to redemption. In chapter 4, we will compare and contrast the Roman Catholic and Protestant views of the sacraments, and then take up the issue of papal infallibility, which, of course, is of great concern for Protestants. Finally, we will consider the division of Roman Catholic theology known as "Mariology," or the study of the place, the role, and the function of the Virgin Mary in the Christian life.

Our task, as I see it, is to be faithful not to our own traditions or even to the heroes of the Reformation. We must be faithful to the truth of Scripture. We love the Reformation because the Reformers loved the truth of God and stood for it so courageously, and in doing so, they brought about a recovery of the purity of the gospel. We should be willing to die for those truths that are absolutely essential to the Christian faith. When the gospel is at stake, we have to "Let goods and kindred go, this mortal life also."[7]

Chapter One

SCRIPTURE

WHEN PROTESTANTS STUDY ROMAN CATHOLIC theology, the accent is usually on the major issue of division between Protestantism and Roman Catholic thought, which is the doctrine of justification. The Protestant position stresses justification by faith alone. I will take up the question of justification in chapter 2, but there is an even more fundamental issue that divides Protestants and Roman Catholics, the issue of Scripture and authority.

The Protestant Reformation of the sixteenth century was so called because it involved a protest against various teachings and practices of Roman Catholicism. However, many who call themselves Protestants today have no clear idea of what the Reformers were protesting. In identifying the key issues involved, historians often point to the so-called *material* cause and the *formal* cause of Reformation. The material cause was the question of justification, how a person ultimately is redeemed by Jesus Christ. The formal issue, which was the underlying issue, the issue that was not in the limelight but nevertheless was at the center of the whole dispute, was the question of authority, specifically the question of the authority of Scripture. It behooves us to begin with an examination of the Roman Catholic understanding of the authority of Scripture, and how it is similar to and different from the Protestant view.

The Reformation battle cry with regard to the material cause was "*sola fide*," that is, "faith alone," while the battle cry with regard to the formal cause was "*sola Scriptura*," that is, "Scripture alone." This was an assertion that the final, ultimate authority for the Christian is the Scriptures alone.

The Protestant Reformation received its initial impetus from the controversy centering around indulgences in Germany. An Augustinian monk by the name of Martin Luther tacked ninety-five theses to the church door at Wittenberg, inviting disputation concerning some abuses that he saw in this program of indulgences. That initial protest mushroomed into a much broader confrontation with Roman Catholic authorities on various points of theology.

Luther participated in several important debates with representatives of the Roman Catholic Church. Perhaps the most important of these was Luther's appearance before Thomas Cardinal Cajetan, the pope's representative to the Imperial Diet (the general assembly of the Holy Roman Empire) of Augsburg in 1518. In this encounter, Luther stated that in his opinion the pope could make mistakes in his ecclesiastical pronouncements. As we will see in chapter 5, this was long before the Roman Catholic Church's formal definition of the infallibility of the pope, which occurred in 1870. Nevertheless, the idea of papal authority was already tacitly assumed within the church. Yet, Luther dared to challenge this idea, insisting that the pope's teachings be documented from Scripture. Likewise, in later debates, particularly the debate at Leipzig with Martin Eck, the master German theologian of the Roman Catholic Church at that time, Luther denied the infallibility of church councils.

Historically, Roman Catholic theologians were divided among themselves as to where the ultimate authority was to be found—in church councils or in papal decisions. Some of them believed the church councils were more authoritative than the popes, and some believed that the popes were more authoritative than the church councils, but Luther denied that either was the highest authority; he said Scripture is the highest authority of all. He did not believe that either councils collectively or popes individually speak infallibly.

This issue came to a head at the Diet of Worms in 1521, when Luther was commanded to stand and defend his cause before the princes of the church and the Holy Roman Emperor Charles V. When he was called to recant his views and his writings, Luther replied, after much consideration: "Unless I am convicted by Scripture and plain reason—I do not accept the authority of popes and councils, for they have contradicted each other—my conscience is captive to the Word of God. I cannot and I will not recant anything, for to go against conscience is neither right nor safe. Here I stand. I cannot do otherwise. God help me. Amen."[1]

The most significant portion of this statement was Luther's insistence on being "convicted by Scripture." He saw the Bible as the ultimate authority. He asserted that both popes and councils could and had erred, but he placed the Scriptures above them, implying that the Bible cannot err. So, the doctrine of Scripture was immediately elevated as a central point for all of the Protestant bodies of the sixteenth century.

A high view of Scripture

Because of this dispute, a caricature has arisen that suggests that Protestantism believes the Bible is the final authority while Roman Catholicism believes that the pope or the church is the final authority, as if Rome had a low view of sacred Scripture. I want to put that caricature to rest as we examine the development of the Roman Catholic view of Scripture.

One of the most important moments in all of Roman Catholic

history was the Council of Trent (1545–63). Trent was called to formulate a response to the Reformation, and it remains the most formidable council of dispute between Protestantism and Roman Catholicism. At this council, Rome gave official definition to its views on justification, the sacraments, and many other issues that were subject to dispute during the Reformation.

In the Fourth Session of the Council of Trent (1546), Rome set forth its definition of Scripture:

> [The gospel], before promised through the prophets in the holy Scriptures, our Lord Jesus Christ, the Son of God, first promulgated with His own mouth, and then commanded to be preached by His Apostles to every creature, as the fountain of all, both saving truth, and moral discipline; and seeing clearly that this truth and discipline are contained in the written books, and the unwritten traditions which, received by the Apostles from the mouth of Christ himself, or from the Apostles themselves, the Holy Ghost dictating, have come down even unto us, transmitted as it were from hand to hand; [the council] following the examples of the orthodox Fathers, receives and venerates with an equal affection of piety, and reverence, all the books both of the Old and of the New Testament—seeing that one God is the author of both.[2]

In this statement, Trent declared that the Scriptures have come to us either directly from the mouth of Christ or from the Apostles under the dictation of God the Holy Spirit. Also, it called God the Author of both the Old and New Testaments. Thus, the Roman Catholic Church set forth a very high view of Scripture.

The most significant word in this statement is *dictating*. The Holy Spirit is said to have dictated the words of Scripture. Evangelical

Christians have often been accused of holding the so-called "dictation theory" of the inspiration of Scripture, which posits that the Holy Spirit dictated the content of Scripture word for word to the human authors, as if He stood over the shoulder of the Apostle Paul and said, "Now write, 'Paul, a servant of Christ Jesus, called to be an apostle, set apart for the gospel of God'" (Rom. 1:1). This view eliminates any contribution of the human authors to the biblical text, leaving no room for individual styles, perspectives, concerns, and so on. For the most part, however, Protestantism has soundly rejected the dictation theory.

But because the word *dictating* appears in the documents of the Council of Trent, critics of Roman Catholic theology have said that Trent taught a crass, simplistic view of inspiration. But Trent did not spell out in detail what it meant by "the Holy Ghost dictating." Furthermore, there is almost universal agreement among Roman Catholic scholars and historians that Trent did not set forth an elaborate notion of dictation. Rather, it was simply using a figurative form of speech to call attention to the fact that the Scriptures have their origin and authority in the power and authority of God, specifically God the Holy Spirit.

If we trace the development of Roman Catholic theology concerning Scripture since the sixteenth century, we see that Rome maintained a very strong view of the inerrancy and inspiration of the Bible. This was particularly evident in the nineteenth century, when the question of the integrity of Scripture was a central issue in both Protestantism and Roman Catholicism during the so-called modernist controversy. This controversy pitted conservative Christians against liberal theologians, who focused much of their effort on attacking the reliability and integrity of the biblical witnesses. The modernist controversy is often seen as a dispute between so-called American fundamentalism and European and American liberalism. However, this controversy was not limited to Protestant circles; it also had a great impact on the Roman Catholic Church. Rome spoke very strongly against the modernist movement in various decrees and papal encyclicals of the nineteenth and early twentieth centuries.

For instance, at Vatican Council I, which met in 1869–70, the Roman Catholic Church said, "These books . . . being written under the inspiration of the Holy Spirit, they have God as their author."3 Furthermore, the council decreed, "they contain revelation without error,"4 a clear affirmation of the idea of biblical inerrancy. This notion of inerrancy was reaffirmed by Pope Pius X in 1907, which was a pivotal year in the so-called modernist controversy. In that year, Pius issued two encyclicals, both of which affirmed the inerrancy and inspiration of Scripture over against modernism, and gave a scathing criticism of the modernist position with respect to Scripture. Also around that time, in order to stem the tide of liberalism, the Roman Catholic Church required each parish priest to give a loyalty oath to the church and to its decrees. That meant that those who were of a modernist persuasion were forced to go underground or to leave the church.

The picture I want to portray is that in the latter decades of the nineteenth century and first decade of the twentieth century, the Roman Catholic Church came down hard against any liberal tendency in dealing with the doctrine of Scripture. It reaffirmed a strong view of Scripture in no uncertain terms. Even Hans Küng (b. 1928), the leading progressive scholar of twentieth-century Roman Catholic theology, said, "From the time of Leo XIII [pope from 1878 to 1903], and particularly during the modernist crisis, the complete and absolute inerrancy of Scripture was explicitly and systematically maintained in papal encyclicals."5 Of course, Küng did not personally affirm inerrancy and believed the church was wrong in its statements. Nevertheless, he had enough scholarly integrity to accurately state what the church was teaching.

An opening for higher criticism

In 1943, Pope Pius XII (pope from 1939 to 1958) released an encyclical titled *Divino Aflante Spiritu* ("Inspired by the Divine Spirit"). This encyclical has proved pivotal in recent discussions as to the latitude scholars have in dealing with the Bible critically. Furthermore, it is of pivotal significance for understanding the current controversy within the Roman Catholic Church with respect to its view of Scripture.

The encyclical began with these words: "Inspired by the Divine Spirit, the Sacred Writers composed those books, which God, in His paternal charity towards the human race, deigned to bestow on them in order 'to teach, to reprove, to correct, to instruct in justice: that the man of God may be perfect, furnished to every good work.'" It went on to describe the Scriptures as a "heaven-sent treasure" and as "the most precious source of doctrine on faith and morals."[6]

Pius then embarked on an interesting historical review of the Roman Catholic Church's previous teachings on Scripture. He accepted and agreed with the formulations of Trent, then added:

> When, subsequently, some Catholic writers, in spite of this solemn definition of Catholic doctrine, by which such divine authority is claimed for the "entire books with all their parts" as to secure freedom from any error whatsoever, ventured to restrict the truth of Sacred Scripture solely to matters of faith and morals, and to regard other matters, whether in the domain of physical science or history, as *"obiter dicta"* and— as they contended—in no wise connected with faith, Our Predecessor of immortal memory, Leo XIII, in the Encyclical Letter *Providentissimus Deus*, published on November 18 in the year 1893, justly and rightly condemned these errors and safe-guarded the studies of the Divine Books by most wise precepts and rules.[7]

I call attention to this portion of *Divino Aflante Spiritu* because Pius looked back over previous encyclicals, including Leo's *Providentissimus Deus* ("God of All Providence"), and condemned as heretical any view of Scripture that tries to restrict its inspiration and inerrancy to matters dealing with faith and morals. In short, he affirmed everything that his predecessors had said. He went on to say: "We, moved by that solicitude for sacred studies, which We manifested from the very beginning of Our Pontificate, have considered that this may most opportunely be done by ratifying and inculcating all that was wisely laid down by Our Predecessor and ordained by His Successors."[8]

He spoke specifically of Leo's work, saying:

The first and greatest care of Leo XIII was to set forth the teaching on the truth of the Sacred Books and to defend it from attack. Hence with grave words did he proclaim that there is no error whatsoever if the sacred writer, speaking of things of the physical order "went by what sensibly appeared" as the Angelic Doctor says, speaking either "in figurative language, or in terms which were commonly used at the time, and which in many instances are in daily use at this day, even among the most eminent men of science."[9]

Pius was indicating here that the doctrine of biblical inerrancy does not mean that there is no room in the Bible for figurative language, for what we Protestants call phenomenological language, language that describes things as they appear to the naked eye, such as a statement that the sun moves across the sky. That is not an error. He then went on to speak of the necessity of very careful textual criticism and of literary analysis of the text of Scripture, so that we might understand the proper forms in which the biblical books come to us. He added:

What is the literal sense of a passage is not always as obvious in the speeches and writings of the ancient authors of the East, as it is in the works of our own time. For what they wished to express is not to be determined by the rules of grammar and philology alone, nor solely by the context; the interpreter must, as it were, go back wholly in spirit to those remote centuries of the East and with the aid of history, archaeology, ethnology, and other sciences, accurately determine what modes of writing, so to speak, the authors of that ancient period would be likely to use, and in fact did use.[10]

Pius was calling for careful investigation of the literary structures of Scripture so that we can understand the forms in which the Word of God was spoken.

This encyclical was pivotal because its tenor, spirit, language, and explicit statements make manifestly obvious that Pius XII had no intention of watering down or weakening in any degree the strong statements Rome already had made regarding the inerrancy of Scripture. In fact, he went to great lengths at the beginning of the encyclical to indicate his agreement with former encyclicals. But because he allowed for an analysis of literary forms in the principle of interpretation, higher critics within Rome jumped to the conclusion that they were free to examine Scripture in terms of the form of myth, the form of legend, the form of saga, and so on. Pius' encyclical opened the door just enough to allow the higher critical movement to begin to function openly within the Roman Catholic Church. That provoked a crisis all of its own, which brings us up to the Second Vatican Council (1962–65).

A restriction of inerrancy?

At Vatican II, there was much agitation over the question of biblical authority and the doctrine of Scripture within the Roman Catholic

Church. After much dispute, the council issued *Dei Verbum* ("the Word of God"), the so-called Dogmatic Constitution on Divine Revelation. It said, "The books of Scripture must be acknowledged as teaching solidly, faithfully and without error that truth which God wanted put into sacred writings for the sake of salvation."[11] The conservatives at the council had been pushing for the inclusion of the term *inerrancy* or the phrase "without error," and here they gained the day. But notice the qualification in this statement. What is it that the books of Scripture are acknowledged as teaching without error? It is "that truth which God wanted put into sacred writings for the sake of salvation." This is not a blanket statement covering all of Scripture. The only subject on which the Scriptures are said to speak inerrantly is salvation.

The conservatives in the Roman Catholic Church looked at the Dogmatic Constitution on Divine Revelation in light of previous church pronouncements on Scripture and said that if Rome is unchanging, infallible, and systematically coherent, the only possible conclusion is that it said nothing new. Rome had already said that Scripture is without error in *all* that it says, meaning that its inerrancy is not limited to truth relevant to salvation. Those who wanted to limit biblical inerrancy to matters of faith and morals were condemned by Pius XII in *Divino Aflante Spiritu* in 1943.

On the other hand, the liberals said the Dogmatic Constitution on Divine Revelation represented progress in the living, breathing vitality of the church. They believed that the constitution did indeed restrict inerrancy to teachings on salvation. They saw it as cracking open the door that *Divino Aflante Spiritu* had firmly closed. Their position reflected what was going on in the background at Vatican II, where Franz Cardinal König, the archbishop of Vienna, declared that the Bible contains errors related to matters of history and natural science. He strongly urged the council not to adopt a rigid view of inerrancy that would not allow scholars to criticize and correct the historical and scientific errors in Scripture. The liberals saw the final statement of the Dogmatic Constitution as a reflection of König's position, but the pope left it unfinalized, saying it was for future generations to study.

So, the conservatives in the Roman Catholic Church believe the question of the inerrancy of Scripture is settled. The liberals disagree, contending that the question is still open for examination.

Positional differences

I have labored this historical survey to show that at least historically, the Roman Catholic Church has had a very high and exalted view of the Scriptures, at least officially and formally. Our task now is to set out the differences between classical Roman Catholic approaches to Scripture and Protestant views. I want to enumerate two very important differences.

The first and most obvious is with respect to the question of the canon. This is a complex question involving not only the number of books that properly belong to the canon but also the method by which the canon was established.

The Roman Catholic Bible contains certain books that are not found in Protestant editions of the Bible. These so-called deutero-canonical books represent a portion of the apocryphal books of the intertestamental period, the centuries between the close of the Old Testament canon and the opening of the New Testament canon. Trent included 1 and 2 Esdras, Tobias, Judith, Ecclesiasticus, Baruch, 1 and 2 Maccabees, and others among the books that are regarded as canonical. These books are denied canonical status by Protestants.

The historical evidence is overwhelming that the Jewish canon did not include these intertestamental books. I would also assert with confidence that the vast majority of Roman Catholic historians and biblical scholars would grant that the historical evidence favors the conclusion that these books were not contained in the Jewish canon. But these facts matter little because of the method by which the Roman Catholic canon was established.

Orthodox Protestants believe that the canon of Scripture is a fallible collection of infallible books. In other words, Protestantism does not believe that the church was infallible in the formation of the canon. We hold that the church was called to make decisions in history as to whether certain books belonged in the canon, and while those decisions were made with much study and passed through a historical sifting, it is conceivable that the church could have made mistakes in what it included or excluded. However, the books that were chosen are regarded as individually infallible. Therefore, as the Westminster Confession of Faith says, the Bible "abundantly [evidences] itself to be the Word of God," preeminently by "the inward work of the Holy Spirit bearing witness by and with the Word in our hearts" (1.5). This means we can be confident that the books in the Protestant canon are the "right" ones.

By contrast, the Roman Catholic Church believes that the Bible is an infallible collection of infallible books. That is, not only are the writings of the writings themselves infallible, but in the process of assembling the canon, the church exercised an infallible ability to recognize and sanction those infallible books.

We can perhaps illustrate the difference between the Protestant and Roman Catholic positions by imagining that God gave us ten books, five of which were infallible and five of which were fallible, containing errors. Then He charged us to separate and identify the infallible books. If we were fallible, we might correctly select four of the five infallible books. However, we also might identify one of the fallible books as infallible. Our decisions, of course, would not change the nature of the books. The one infallible book we did not select would still be infallible, even though we failed to include it in our "canon." Likewise, the fallible book we picked would not therefore be infallible. Our decisions would have no effect in this way because we are fallible.

Of course, if we were infallible, we would correctly identify the five infallible books, leaving none out and including none of the fallible books. We would make no mistakes because we would have the infallible ability to recognize infallibility. This is the ability Rome claims for its historical selection and collection of the books of Scripture.

So, the historical question of whether the Jewish canon contained certain books is ultimately irrelevant to Rome, because the church is sure that it has the right books because it could not help but select the right books due to its infallible power of recognition.

Second, the central issue of division with respect to Scripture is the relationship of Scripture and the tradition of the church. Earlier, I noted the declaration from the Fourth Session of the Council of Trent, which says, "[The gospel], before promised through the prophets in the holy Scriptures, our Lord Jesus Christ, the Son of God, first promulgated with His own mouth, and then commanded to be preached by His Apostles to every creature, as the fountain of all, both saving truth, and moral discipline; and seeing clearly that this truth and discipline are contained in the written books, and the unwritten traditions. . . ."[12] So, Trent affirmed that the truth of God is contained both in the written documents that make up the canon and in the unwritten traditions. This raises the issue of the dual-source theory of revelation. Are there two sources of revelation—Scripture and tradition—or is there only one source—Scripture?

The Protestant view is *sola Scriptura*, that is, "Scripture alone." God's special revelation comes only in the Scriptures. Other books may be of value for instruction. Even the apocrypha is helpful to the church, though it is not revelatory. But the Roman Catholic Church historically recognizes two sources of revelation, Scripture and tradition.

This issue centered on the declarations of the Council of Trent, as well as statements made in twentieth-century debates on the point. With the advance of the so-called *nouvelle théologie*, "the new theology," in the progressive wing of the Roman Catholic Church, there were some within Rome who wanted to get away from the dual-source theory of revelation. Oddly enough, the issue was provoked by an Anglican scholar, who, while doing doctoral research on the historical background of the Council of Trent, stumbled on some significant information. He noticed that the first draft of the Fourth Session of Trent said that the truth of God is found partly in Scripture and partly in tradition. This draft repeated a certain Latin word—*partim, partim*—indicating that revelation was partly in Scripture, partly in tradition. That clearly indicated that there are two sources of revelation. However, the final draft did not have the words *partim, partim*, but merely the word *et*, or "and," as it said the truth of God is contained in Scripture and in tradition.[13]

The question is why the council changed the document's wording, dropping the *partim, partim* formulation in favor of *et*, which is more ambiguous. If the truth of God is contained in Scripture and tradition, can we say that the truth of God is contained in Scripture and in the Westminster Confession of Faith? As a Presbyterian, I believe that the Westminster Confession gives a very accurate reproduction of Christian truth, and the truth of God is contained in it because Scripture is quoted and expounded there. However, I do not think the confession is inspired or inerrant. Likewise, I think the truth of God can be found in a sermon or in a lecture, but not that it finds its origin there. So *et* could indicate that the truth of God is found in Scripture and in tradition, but that tradition is not a source of revelation.

Further study revealed that when the first draft of the Fourth Session came before the assembly, two Roman Catholic theologians got to their feet and protested the use of *partim, partim*. They objected on the grounds that to use this language would destroy the uniqueness and sufficiency of Holy Scripture. At that point, the council session was interrupted by war. The records of the council's debate at the Fourth Session end at that point, so we do not know why the words *partim, partim* were changed to *et*. Did the council bend to the protest of the two scholars or was it simply left as a studied ambiguity?

J. R. Geiselmann, who was a leader of the new left in the Roman Catholic Church in the mid-twentieth century, insisted that the change from *partim, partim* to *et* at Trent meant the Roman Catholic Church had done away with the idea of two sources of revelation. Heinrich Lennerz, a conservative scholar in the Roman Catholic Church, said the change was merely stylistic, having no theological significance. Bolstering his argument is the fact that the church after Trent assumed the dual-source theory, and multiple sources of revelation are mentioned in papal encyclicals as late as *Humani Generis* ("Of the Human Race," 1950). So, this is a burning issue within Roman Catholic theology.

Roman Catholic and Protestant affirmations

The words of the most recent Catechism of the Catholic Church (1995) reflect Rome's views on these issues of Scripture vs. tradition and the books that comprise the canon (numbers in parentheses indicate the section of the catechism that is being cited):

> "Sacred Tradition and Sacred Scripture, then, are bound closely together, and communicate one with the other. For both of them, flowing out from the same divine well-spring, come together in some fashion to form one thing, and move towards the same goal." Each of them makes present and fruitful in the Church the mystery of Christ, who promised to remain with his own "always, to the close of the age." (Section 80)

> "Sacred Scripture is the speech of God as it is put down in writing under the breath of the Holy Spirit." "And [Holy] Tradition transmits in its entirety the Word of God which

has been entrusted to the apostles by Christ the Lord and the Holy Spirit. It transmits it to the successors of the apostles so that, enlightened by the Spirit of truth, they may faithfully preserve, expound and spread it abroad by their preaching." (81)

As a result the Church, to whom the transmission and interpretation of Revelation is entrusted, "does not derive her certainty about all revealed truths from the holy Scriptures alone. Both Scripture and Tradition must be accepted and honoured with equal sentiments of devotion and reverence." (82)

It was by the apostolic Tradition that the Church discerned which writings are to be included in the list of the sacred books.

This complete list is called the canon of Scripture. It includes 46 books for the Old Testament (45 if we count Jeremiah and Lamentations as one) and 27 for the New.

The Old Testament: Genesis, Exodus, Leviticus, Numbers, Deuteronomy, Joshua, Judges, Ruth, 1 and 2 Samuel, 1 and 2 Kings, 1 and 2 Chronicles, Ezra and Nehemiah, Tobit, Judith, Esther, 1 and 2 Maccabees, Job, Psalms, Proverbs, Ecclesiastes, the Song of Songs, the Wisdom of Solomon, Sirach (Ecclesiasticus), Isaiah, Jeremiah, Lamentations, Baruch, Ezekiel, Daniel, Hosea, Joel, Amos, Obadiah, Jonah, Micah, Nahum, Habakkuk, Zephaniah, Haggai, Zachariah and Malachi.

The New Testament: the Gospels according to Matthew, Mark, Luke and John, the Acts of the Apostles, the Letters of St. Paul to the Romans, 1 and 2 Corinthians, Galatians,

Ephesians, Philippians, Colossians, 1 and 2 Thessalonians, 1 and 2 Timothy, Titus, Philemon, the Letter to the Hebrews, the Letters of James, 1 and 2 Peter, 1, 2 and 3 John, and Jude, and Revelation (the Apocalypse). (120)[14]

By contrast, one of the great Reformation doctrinal statements, the Westminster Confession of Faith, which deals with the doctrine of Scripture in its first chapter, lists the sixty-six books of the Protestant Bible as those that constitute the canon (1.2), saying:

The books commonly called Apocrypha, not being of divine inspiration, are no part of the Canon of Scripture; and therefore are of no authority in the Church of God, nor to be any otherwise approved, or made use of, than other human writings. (1.3)

The confession then adds:

The authority of the holy Scripture, for which it ought to be believed and obeyed, dependeth not upon the testimony of any man or Church, but wholly upon God (who is truth itself), the Author thereof; and therefore it is to be received, because it is the Word of God. (1.4)

The Supreme Judge, by which all controversies of religion are to be determined, and all decrees of councils, opinions of ancient writers, doctrines of men, and private spirits, are to be examined, and in whose sentence we are to rest, can be no other but the Holy Spirit speaking in the Scripture. (1.10)

Thus, the disagreement over Scripture in the sixteenth century persists today, forming an insurmountable barrier to union between

Protestantism and Rome. If Protestants and Roman Catholics could agree that there is but one source of revelation, the Scriptures (minus the apocryphal books in the Roman Catholic Bible), we could then sit down and discuss the meaning of the biblical texts. But ever since Trent, all the efforts to have biblical discussions between Protestants and Roman Catholics have come to dead ends when they encountered a papal encyclical or a conciliar statement.

For instance, involved in the controversy over Scripture and authority was the conflict over the Protestant doctrine of the private interpretation of Scripture, which teaches that every Christian has the right to interpret the Bible for himself or herself. However, this "right" does not include the freedom to misinterpret Scripture. Before God, we do not have the right to be wrong. With the right of private interpretation comes the responsibility to interpret the Bible correctly, not turning the Bible into a lump of clay that can be twisted, shaped, and distorted to fit our own biases.

In response to the Protestant claim of private interpretation, Rome declared at the Fourth Session of Trent: "Furthermore, in order to restrain petulant spirits, [the council] decrees, that no one, relying on his own skill, shall,—in matters of faith, and of morals pertaining to the edification of Christian doctrine,—wresting the sacred Scripture to his own senses, presume to interpret the said sacred Scripture contrary to that sense which holy mother Church,—whose it is to judge of the true sense and interpretation of the holy Scriptures,—hath held and doth hold."[5] In other words, Trent declared that Rome's interpretation of Scripture is the only correct interpretation. When a Protestant presents a biblical interpretation, if it differs from Rome's official interpretation, further talk is pointless, because the Roman Catholics simply say the Protestant is wrong. The tradition of the church is sacrosanct at that point.

Chapter Two

JUSTIFICATION

I HAVE FOUND THAT THE vast majority of people who call themselves Protestants have no idea what they are protesting. If I ask them, "Why are you Protestant rather than Roman Catholic?" they will say, "Well, I don't believe I need to confess my sins to a priest," or, "I don't believe the pope is infallible," or, "I don't believe in the bodily assumption of the Virgin Mary into heaven," or something of that sort. These are not inconsequential matters, of course, but they do not get to the heart of the reason why Protestants separated from the Roman Catholic Church.

When Desiderius Erasmus wrote his *Diatribe* against Martin Luther, Luther actually thanked Erasmus for not attacking him on matters that Luther considered to be trivial; rather, Erasmus addressed the core issue of the Reformation, which was the question of how a sinner finds salvation in Christ. Luther asserted that the doctrine of justification by faith alone is the article upon which the church stands or falls. As we saw in the previous chapter, the formal cause of the Reformation was the question of Scripture, but the material cause was the question of justification. We should not get bogged down in extraneous issues that perhaps could have been resolved with further meetings and discussions, but focus on the issue that was the point over which Christendom was severely fractured and fragmented, as it remains to this day.

Part of the disagreement over justification stems from the meaning of the word *justification* itself. The English word *justification* is derived from the Latin term *justificare*, which literally means "to make righteous." The early Latin fathers, who studied the Scriptures by means of the Vulgate (the fourth-century Latin translation of the Bible) rather than the Septuagint (the Greek translation of the Old Testament) and the Greek New Testament, developed their doctrine of justification based on their understanding of the legal system of the Roman Empire. In time, the doctrine of justification came to address the question of how an unrighteous person, a fallen sinner, can be made righteous. In the development of the doctrine of justification in Rome, the idea emerged that justification occurs after sanctification. That is, in order to be declared just, we first must be sanctified to the point that we exhibit a righteousness that is acceptable to God.

The Protestant Reformation, which followed the revival of the study of antiquities, focused attention on the Greek meaning of the concept of justification, which was the word *dikaioo*, which means "to declare righteous" rather than "to make righteous." So, in Protestantism, justification was understood to come before the process of sanctification. Therefore, very early on, there was a complete difference of understanding regarding the order of salvation between the two communions.

Grace received, lost, regained

From the Roman perspective, justification is a function of the sacerdotal operations of the church; that is, justification takes place primarily through the use of the sacraments, beginning with the sacrament of baptism. Rome says that the sacrament of baptism, among others, functions *ex opere operato*, which literally means "through the working of the work." Protestants have understood this to mean that baptism works, as it were, automatically. If a person is baptized, that person is automatically placed in a state of grace or in the state of justification. The Roman Catholic Church is quick to say it does not like to use the word *automatic*, because there has to be a certain predisposition in the recipient of baptism; at the very least, he or she must have no hostility toward the reception of the sacrament in order for it to function. In any case, Rome has a high view of the efficacy of baptism to bring a person into a state of grace. This is because, in the sacrament of baptism, grace is said to be *infused* or poured into the soul.

Let me say a word about this concept of infusion. Protestants believe that a person is justified when the righteousness of Christ is imputed or credited to his account. We likewise believe that our sins were imputed to Christ on the cross, that is, they were placed in His account, and He paid for them. So Protestants see a double imputation. But Rome believes in infusion, which is the view that the righteousness of Christ is actually put into the believer, so that the person is actually righteous. The righteousness of Christ is not simply credited to the person's account; it actually becomes the person's possession.

The Council of Trent, where the Roman Catholic Church defined its position in relation to the protests of the Reformers, used the terms *cooperare et assentare*, meaning that believers must "cooperate with and assent to" the grace that is bestowed on them in baptism. The council said: "The Synod furthermore declares, that in adults, the beginning of the said Justification is to be derived from the prevenient grace of God, through Jesus Christ, that is to say, from His vocation, whereby, without any merits existing on their parts, they are called; that so they, who by sins were alienated from

God, may be disposed through His quickening and assisting grace, to convert themselves to their own justification, by freely assenting to and co-operating with that said grace."[1] So, if someone assents to the infused grace of baptism and cooperates with it, he or she is then in a state of grace or justification.

However, the grace that is received through infusion is by no means immutable. When Roman Catholics speak of their sacramental theology, they use quantitative terms with respect to grace, saying that there can be an increase or a diminution of it. In other words, a baptized person can lose some of his infused grace. In fact, it may be lost entirely, removing the person from a state of justification and putting him or her under the threat of damnation.

This loss of saving grace takes place when the person commits a particular type of sin—a mortal sin. Roman Catholic theology distinguishes venial sins and mortal sins, with mortal sins being more egregious. However, there is no universal agreement as to which sins are mortal sins. Many catalogs have been produced that delineate various sins as being serious enough to be considered mortal. In any case, mortal sin is so named because it is serious enough to cause the death of the justifying grace that was infused to a person at baptism.

In the sixteenth century, John Calvin criticized the Roman Catholic distinction between mortal and venial sins. He did not deny that there are gradations of sin, noting that the New Testament recognizes that some sins are more serious than others (see Rom. 1:28–31; 1 Cor. 6:9–10; Eph. 5:3–5). But Calvin said that all sin is mortal in that it deserves death. At creation, God told Adam and Eve not to eat from the tree of the knowledge of good and evil, "for in the day that you eat of it you shall surely die" (Gen. 2:17). Likewise, He said through the prophet Ezekiel, "the soul who sins shall die" (18:4b). This means that even the smallest sin is an act of treason against God's sovereign rule and therefore deserving of death. But Calvin went on to say that while every sin is mortal in the sense that it deserves death, no sin is mortal in the sense that it destroys the saving grace that a Christian receives upon his or her justification.[2]

According to Roman Catholic theology, if a person who has been baptized and has received the infused grace of justification commits a mortal sin and thereby destroys that justifying grace, all is not lost. There is a way by which that person's justification can be restored. This restoration of justification also happens via a sacrament. In this case, it is the sacrament of penance, which the Roman Catholic Church in the sixteenth century defined as "a second plank" of justification for those who have made shipwreck of their souls, that is, those who have committed mortal sins and lost the grace of justification.[3] The sacrament of penance was at the heart of the problem that erupted in the sixteenth century, because penance had several elements, including contrition, confession and then acts of satisfaction, demonstrating that one's confession was not moved merely out of a fear of punishment but out of a genuine sorrow for having offended God.

Confession, of course, was followed by priestly absolution, whereby the priest would say to the penitent person, "*Te absolvo*," or, "I absolve you." At this point, many misunderstandings and caricatures have arisen among Protestants. We often say: "I don't have to confess my sins to a priest; I can confess directly to God. I don't have to have a priest tell me that I'm absolved of my sin." We tend to aim our critiques at the ritual elements involved in the sacrament of penance. But not all of the Reformers were opposed to confession. For instance, the Lutherans carried on the act of confession because the New Testament says that we are to confess our sins one to another (James 5:16). They believe that it is salutary for a Christian to confess his sins in a situation where that confession is protected by the discretion of the minister, and the minister has the authority to declare the assurance of God's pardon to those who are genuinely sorry for their sins.

So, for the Reformers, confession was not the issue. Rather, it was the next step in the sacrament of penance. In order to be restored to a state of grace, the repentant sinner has to perform works of satisfaction. This step also is subject to Protestant misunderstandings and caricatures. If you ask a Protestant the difference between Protestantism and Roman Catholicism, the Protestant will typically say: "We believe that justification is by faith but Roman Catholics say it is by works. We believe it is by grace but Roman Catholics say it is by merit. We believe it is through Christ but Roman Catholics believe it is through one's own righteousness." These are terrible slanders against Rome. From the sixteenth century to today, the Roman Catholic Church has said that justification requires faith, the grace of God, and the work of Jesus Christ. The debate arose because Protestants said justification is by faith *alone*, whereas Rome said justification requires faith *plus* works, grace *plus* merit, Christ *plus* inherent righteousness. It was those pluses that became so problematic in the sixteenth century, particularly with respect to the works of satisfaction that were part of the sacrament of penance.

Rome teaches that works of satisfaction produce merit, but it makes a sharp distinction between kinds of merit. Condign merit is so meritorious it demands a reward. God would be unjust if He did not reward works that were condignly meritorious. However, the merit that is acquired through works of satisfaction in the sacrament of penance do not rise to the level of condign merit; these works produce congruous merit. This is real merit, but it is dependent on previous grace. It simply makes it congruous, or fitting, for God to restore the person to a state of grace. So, if a person goes through the sacrament of penance and does the works of satisfaction prescribed by the priest, it is congruous or fitting for God to restore that person to a state of justification.

Of course, Luther saw the New Testament teaching of justification by faith alone as a thunderbolt against any kind of merit, condign or congruous. He believed that people should never be taught that any work they do can add in any way to the satisfaction for our sins that was accomplished by Christ. Nevertheless, Rome continued to teach that works are involved in justification.

Decrees and condemnations

The Roman Catholic Church responded to the Protestant criticisms at the Council of Trent, where it gave official, formal decrees with respect to its doctrine. Justification was discussed in the Sixth Session, and the church laid out a number of decrees regarding its view, as well as thirty-three specific condemnations, or "anathemas," of different views, which Rome regarded as repudiations of error and heresy. Each of these condemnations was couched in a consistent formula: "If anyone saith . . . let him be anathema," which means, "let him be damned."

The vast majority of these condemnations were directed at the Reformers, but in many cases, they missed their mark. There were certain misunderstandings implied in the anathemas. For this reason, some have said the whole disagreement was a misunderstanding and the two sides were simply talking past each other. That is true to a degree, but some of the condemnations were right on the mark, as they clearly anathematized the Reformation doctrine of justification by faith alone.

That is significant. If the Reformation articulation of the biblical doctrine of justification was correct (and I, of course, believe that it was), to anathematize it was to anathematize the gospel. If any communion claims to be Christian but denies or condemns an essential truth of Christianity, at that point that organization shows itself to be apostate and no longer a true or valid church. This is part of the problem with the ongoing discussions between Rome and Protestant bodies. Many Protestant groups do not care deeply about doctrinal differences, so they are happy to enter into discussions and ecumenical agreements with Rome. But if we take the biblical doctrine of justification seriously, there can be no rapprochement on that point. There can be no unity unless one side surrenders, because the two positions are simply incompatible. Someone is right and someone is wrong, and the one who has significantly distorted the New Testament gospel deserves condemnation. As the Apostle Paul said to the Galatians, "But even if we or an angel from heaven should preach to you a gospel contrary to the one we preached to you, let him be accursed" (1:8). So, one side or the other, Protestantism or Roman Catholicism, *deserves* to be under the anathema of God.

The condemnations of the Sixth Session of Trent are very serious, but I believe the first section, wherein Rome defined its doctrine of justification, is even more problematic. Rome went to great lengths to define saving faith and what it involves. As I said earlier, it is a slanderous caricature to say that Protestants believe in justification by faith and Roman Catholics believe in justification by works, as if faith were not necessary. Rather, Rome clearly taught in the Sixth Session of Trent that faith is a necessary condition for justification. As I mentioned in the introduction, Trent declared that faith is the *initium*, the *fundamentum*, and the *radix* of justification. These terms mean that faith is the beginning of justification, the starting place, that which initiates justification. Likewise, it is the foundation, the fundamental structure on which justification is established, without which foundation there could be no justification. Finally, faith is also the root, the radical core of justification.

With these affirmations, Rome was saying that faith is no mere appendage to justification. Rather, it is a condition without which justification cannot follow. However, according to Rome, faith is not a *sufficient* condition. A sufficient condition is one that, if met, will surely lead to the desired result. Oxygen, for example, is in most cases a necessary condition for fire. But it is not a sufficient condition. If there is no oxygen there will be no fire, but even if there is abundant oxygen there will not necessarily be fire, because oxygen does not have sufficient power to cause a fire.

The Council of Trent taught that faith is not sufficient in and of itself to yield the result of justification. In its explanation of the loss of justification through mortal sin, it explicitly declared that a person in possession of saving faith can commit mortal sin. According to Rome, when a person commits mortal sin while in possession of true faith, faith is not lost but justification is. Thus, a person can have saving faith without justification. He can retain the faith but lose the justification by committing a mortal sin.

The instrumental cause: baptism or faith?

It is also important that we understand how Rome views the instrumental cause of justification. We generally think of causality in one-dimensional terms, but the Roman Catholic Church distinguishes several types of causes. These distinctions go back to the medieval synthesis between Roman Catholic theology and the teachings of the ancient Greek philosopher Aristotle.

Aristotle created a famous illustration to distinguish various kinds of causes. He imagined a sculptor creating a statue from a chunk of marble. The material cause of the statue is the marble from which it is made. A sculpture of marble is impossible without the marble, so the material from which the statue is sculpted is the material cause. The formal cause of the statue is the artist's sketch depicting his vision of the finished statue; this would be his blueprint, as it were. The final cause is the purpose for which the statue is made—perhaps it is intended to beautify someone's garden. The efficient cause is that which actually transforms the material into a statue, which is the work of the sculptor himself.

Aristotle also identified the instrumental cause, which is the instruments that the sculptor uses to create the statue. A sculptor does not approach a block of marble with a picture of the finished statue in his mind and simply tell the material to transform into the statue. The sculptor has to begin to chip away at the stone with his hammer and chisel in order to shape it into a piece of art. Those tools are the instrumental cause of the statue.

When the Roman Catholic theologians applied Aristotle's thinking on causes to the doctrine of justification, they identified the instrumental cause of justification—the tool by which a person is brought into a state of grace—as the sacrament of baptism. The Reformers disagreed strongly, saying that the instrumental cause is faith, not the sacrament. The Reformers affirmed that the instrument by which we are linked to the work of Christ for our salvation is faith alone. So, the question of the instrumental cause of justification was no small issue at the time of the Reformation.

The Roman Catholic view of justification is what is known as an analytical view. An analytical statement is one that is inherently true. The statement "Two plus two equals four" is an analytical statement: it expresses a formal truth. That is, if we examine what "two plus two" means, we find that it means the same thing that we see on the other side of the equation, which is "four." This is a mathematical truth, not something that has to be confirmed by experimentation or observation. Here is another example of an analytical statement: "A bachelor is an unmarried man." In this statement, we learn nothing in the predicate that is not in the subject. The statement tells us nothing that defines the term *bachelor* further than the word itself.

Both Protestants and Roman Catholics agree that in the final analysis, no one is justified unless God declares that person just, and that declaration of God is a legal declaration by His own judgment. When we say that the Roman view is analytical, we mean that God will not say that a person is just unless that person, under analysis, is found to be actually just. He does not count people who are not really just as just. This is why Rome said in the sixteenth century that before God will declare someone justified, righteousness must inhere within his soul. Righteousness must be inherent within the person; God must examine his life and find righteousness there. If a person dies in mortal sin, he goes to hell. If the person dies with any sin, with any imperfection or blemish on his soul, he cannot be admitted into heaven but must first go through the purging fires of purgatory, where his impurities are cleansed away until such time as righteousness is truly inherent in him.

Much is at stake here. One of the most significant theological issues we can ever discuss is on the table. It is the question of what we must do to be saved. If I thought that I had to arrive at a state, no matter how much grace the church has for me, of pure righteousness without any imperfections in order to reach heaven, I would completely despair of ever having salvation. If my church taught this concept of justification, that would be horrible news, not good news. Thankfully, the Reformation affirmed the biblical gospel, the truth that the moment a person possesses saving faith, he is transferred from the kingdom of darkness into the kingdom of light, his sins are taken away, he is declared to be just on the basis of the righteousness of Christ, and he is adopted into the family of God. There is no need for inherent righteousness, for purgatory, or for a second plank of justification.

The Reformation view of justification

The motto of the Reformation with respect to the doctrine of justification was *sola fide*, which means "faith alone." This was one of five great Reformation slogans, including *sola Scriptura* ("Scripture alone," which we examined in the previous chapter), *sola gratia* ("grace alone"), *solus Christus* ("Christ alone"), and *soli Deo gloria* ("to God alone be the glory").

As we have seen, the Roman Catholic Church also strongly affirms that faith is necessary for justification. In fact, we saw that it was a necessary condition but not a sufficient condition. A person cannot have justification without faith, but he can have faith without justification. So, the point of the controversy between the magisterial Reformers and Rome focused on this word *sola*, by which the Reformers asserted that justification is by faith alone.

Sometimes a motto or slogan can oversimplify matters to a great degree, and this happens sometimes with *sola fide*. People ask me, "Isn't it also necessary for a person to repent in order to be justified?" I always tell them that repentance is absolutely necessary. But the Reformers understood repentance to be an integral part of that faith that justifies (though we may distinguish it from faith in one sense). *Sola fide* is simply shorthand for the idea that justification is by Christ alone, that when we put our faith in what Jesus has done for us, we receive justification.

So, we can set forth the different formulas from the sixteenth century. The Roman Catholic view is something like this: faith + works = justification. The Protestant view, which I believe is the biblical view, is that faith = justification + works. The Reformers placed works on the far side of the equation, opposite faith, because whatever works we do as Christians add absolutely nothing to the ground of our justification. In other words, God does not declare us just because of any works that we do. It is by faith alone that we receive the gift of justification.

The Apostle Paul says: "Now we know that whatever the law says it speaks to those who are under the law, so that every mouth may be stopped, and the whole world may be held accountable to God. For by works of the law no human being will be justified in his sight, since through the law comes knowledge of sin" (Rom. 3:19–20). Then, explaining the doctrine of justification more fully, he sets it in contrast with the concept of justification through the works of the law:

But now the righteousness of God has been manifested apart from the law, although the Law and the Prophets bear witness to it—the righteousness of God through faith in Jesus Christ for all who believe. For there is no distinction: for all have sinned and fall short of the glory of God, and are justified by his grace as a gift, through the redemption that is in Christ Jesus, whom God put forward as a propitiation by his blood, to be received by faith. This was to show God's righteousness, because in his divine forbearance he had passed over former sins. It was to show his righteousness at the present time, so that he might be just and the justifier of the one who has faith in Jesus. (Vv. 21–26)

At the very heart of the controversy in the sixteenth century was the question of the ground by which God declares anyone righteous in His sight. The psalmist asked, "If you, O LORD, should mark iniquities, O Lord, who could stand?" (Ps. 130:3). In other words, if we have to stand before God and face His perfect justice and perfect judgment of our performance, none of us would be able to pass review. We all would fall, because as Paul reiterates, all of us have fallen short of the glory of God (Rom. 3:23). So, the pressing question of justification is how can an unjust person ever be justified in the presence of a righteous and holy God?

As I mentioned previously, the Roman Catholic view is known as analytical justification. This means that God will declare a person just only when, under His perfect analysis, He finds that he *is* just, that righteousness is inherent in him. The person cannot have that righteousness without faith, without grace, and without the assistance of Christ. Nevertheless, in the final analysis, true righteousness must be present in the soul of a person before God will ever declare him just.

Whereas the Roman view is analytical, the Reformation view is that justification is synthetic. A synthetic statement is one in which something new is added in the predicate that is not contained in the subject. If I said to you, "The bachelor was a poor man," I have told you something new in the second part of the sentence that was not already contained in the word *bachelor*. All bachelors are men by definition, but not all bachelors are poor men. There are many wealthy bachelors. Poverty and wealth are concepts that are not inherent in the idea of bachelorhood. So, when we say, "The bachelor was a poor man," there is a synthesis, as it were.

When we say that the Reformation view of justification is synthetic, we mean that when God declares a person to be just in His sight, it is not because of what He finds in that person under His analysis. Rather, it is on the basis of something that is added to the person. That something that is added, of course, is the righteousness of Christ. This is why Luther said that the righteousness by which we are justified is *extra nos*, meaning "apart from us" or "outside of us." He also called it an "alien righteousness," not a righteousness that properly belongs to us, but a righteousness that is foreign to us, alien to us. It comes from outside the sphere of our own behavior. With both of these terms, Luther was speaking about the righteousness of Christ.

The importance of imputation

If any word was at the center of the firestorm of the Reformation controversy and remains central to the debate even in our day, it is *imputation*. Numerous meetings were held between Protestants and Roman Catholics to try to repair the schism that was taking place in the sixteenth century. Theologians from Rome met with the magisterial Reformers, trying to resolve the difficulties and preserve the unity of the church. There was a longing for such unity on both sides. But the one concept that was always a sticking point, the idea that was so precious to the Protestants and such a stumbling block for the Roman Catholics, was imputation. We cannot really understand what the Reformation was about without understanding the central importance of this concept.

When Paul explains the doctrine of justification, he cites the example of the patriarch Abraham. He writes: "For what does the Scripture say? 'Abraham believed God, and it was accounted to him for righteousness'" (Rom. 4:3, citing Gen. 15:6). In other words, Abraham had faith, and therefore God justified him. Abraham was still a sinner. The rest of the history of the life of Abraham reveals that he did not always obey God. Nevertheless, God counted him righteous because he believed in the promise God had made to him. This is an example of imputation, which involves transferring something legally to someone's account, to reckon something to be there. So, Paul speaks of God counting Abraham as righteous or reckoning him as righteous, even though, in and of himself, Abraham was not yet righteous. He did not have righteousness inhering in him.

As I noted above, the Roman Catholic idea is that grace is infused into the soul of a person at baptism, making the person inherently righteous, so that God therefore judges him to be righteous. But the Reformers insisted that we are justified when God imputes someone else's righteousness to our account, namely, the righteousness of Christ.

If any statement summarizes and captures the essence of the Reformation view, it is Luther's famous Latin formula *simul justus et peccator*. *Simul* is the word from which we get the English *simultaneous*; it means "at the same time." *Justus* is the Latin word for "just" or "righteous." *Et* simply means "and." *Peccator* means "sinner." So, with this formula— "at the same time just and sinner"—Luther was saying that in our justification, we are at the same time righteous and sinful. Now, if he had said we are just and sinful at the same time *and* in the same relationship, that would have been a contradiction in terms. But that is not what he was saying. He was saying that, in one sense, we are just. In another sense, we are sinners. In and of ourselves, under God's scrutiny, we still have sin. But by God's imputation of the righteousness of Jesus Christ to our accounts, we are considered just.

This is the very heart of the gospel. In order to get into heaven, will I be judged by my righteousness or by the righteousness of Christ? If I have to trust in my righteousness to get into heaven, I must completely and utterly despair of any possibility of ever being redeemed. But when we see that the righteousness that is ours by faith is the perfect righteousness of Christ, we see how glorious is the good news of the gospel. The good news is simply this: I can be reconciled to God. I can be justified, not on the basis of what I do, but on the basis of what has been accomplished for me by Christ.

Of course, Protestantism really teaches a double imputation. Our sin is imputed to Jesus and His righteousness is imputed to us. In this twofold transaction, we see that God does not compromise His integrity in providing salvation for His people. Rather, He punishes sin fully after it has been imputed to Jesus. This is why He is able to be both "just and the justifier of the one who has faith in Jesus," as Paul writes in Romans 3:26. So, my sin goes to Jesus and His righteousness comes to me. This is a truth worth dividing the church. This is the article on which the church stands or falls, because it is the article on which we all stand or fall.

It is strange to me that Rome reacted so negatively to the idea of imputation, because in its own doctrine of the atonement, it holds that our sins are imputed to Jesus on the cross, which is why His atoning death has value for us. The principle of imputation is there. Furthermore, Rome teaches that a sinner can receive indulgences through the transfer of merit from the treasury of merit, but this transfer cannot be accomplished except by imputation.

The Roman Catholic Church declared that the Reformation view of justification involves God in a "legal fiction" that undermines His integrity. Rome was asking how God, in His perfect righteousness and holiness, can declare a sinner to be just if he is not, in fact, just. That seems to involve God in a fictional declaration. The Protestant response was that God declares people just because He imputes the real righteousness of Christ to them. There is nothing fictional about Christ's righteousness, and there is nothing fictional about God's gracious imputation of that righteousness.

Paul versus James

Rome's principal objection to the Protestant view of justification was based on the teaching of James. In his epistle, James writes: "Was not Abraham our father justified by works when he offered up his son Isaac on the altar? . . . The Scripture was fulfilled that says, 'Abraham believed God, and it was counted to him as righteousness'—and he was called a friend of God. You see that a person is justified by works and not by faith alone" (2:21, 23–24). On the surface, it seems that James is teaching that works are involved in justification. How are we to understand this passage?

When scholars consider the difference between Paul's teaching in Romans 3, 4, and 5, and James' teaching in chapter 2, they look at it in different ways. Some say that the book of James was written before the epistle to the Romans, and one of the things on Paul's agenda in writing Romans was to correct the mistake that James taught in his epistle. Others say Romans was written first and then James, and part of James' agenda was to offer a corrective to the erroneous teaching of the Apostle Paul. Others say it does not matter who wrote first or second, this is simply evidence that the Apostles of the first century had different theologies, and that no consistent, monolithic view of justification is to be found in the New Testament. But those who believe that the Bible is the Word of God and that both the book of Romans and the book of James are inspired by the Holy Spirit cannot get off the hook so easily. They are faced with the difficult task of reconciling the two books.

It would be nice to say that when James and Paul speak of justification, James uses one Greek word and Paul uses a different Greek word. However, both of them use the same Greek word, *dikaioo*. It would be nice to say that James uses one patriarch as an example of his viewpoint and Paul uses a different patriarch to support his viewpoint. However, both Paul and James use Abraham as exhibit A to bolster their views. So, the more we look at this, the more the plot thickens and the more difficult it seems to be to reconcile the two passages.

In order to see how these passages fit together, we have to keep two very important points in mind. First, while both passages refer to Abraham, Paul cites an event from Abraham's life that is recorded in Genesis 15. This event occurred long before Abraham went to sacrifice his son Isaac on the altar. So, from Genesis 15 and onward, Abraham was already in a state of justification. By contrast, James refers specifically to Abraham's obedience in his willingness to sacrifice Isaac, which is recorded in Genesis 22. So, when James is talking about Abraham's justification, he is referring primarily to the action that takes place in Genesis 22, whereas Paul is laboring the point that Abraham was justified freely, without having done any work.

But the real resolution to the difficulty comes when we ask ourselves whether Paul and James are addressing the same question. James asks: "What good is it, my brothers, if someone says he has faith but does not have works? Can that faith save him? If a brother or sister is poorly clothed and lacking in daily food, and one of you says to them, 'Go in peace, be warmed and filled,' without giving them the things needed for the body, what good is that? So also faith by itself, if it does not have works, is dead" (2:14–17). So, James is asking, "If someone says he has faith but has no works to verify his profession of faith, can that kind of faith save him?"

The answer, of course, is no. As Luther declared, "We are justified by faith alone, but not by a faith that is alone." If the faith that we profess is a naked faith with no evidence of works, it is not saving faith. It is, as James says, a "dead" faith, not a living faith. A living faith shows its life by obedience. Such works of obedience contribute nothing to our justification, but if the works are not present, that absence is proof positive that justification has not occurred.

James goes on to write: "But someone will say, 'You have faith and I have works.' Show me your faith apart from your works, and I will show you my faith by my works" (v. 18). Here we see that the issue that is on James' mind is the manifestation of faith. But to whom are we to show our faith? Does God need to see our works to know whether our professions of faith are genuine? Of course not. God knew that Abraham possessed saving faith all the way back in Genesis 15, long before he proved himself willing to sacrifice Isaac. And Paul labors the point that once authentic faith was present, God counted him righteous. However, other people cannot see what is in our hearts unless we demonstrate what is there. If I say that I have faith, how can I demonstrate the truth of my profession other than by my obedience, by my manifestation of works?

When James uses this term, he is talking about justifying a claim to faith before men. Jesus Himself used the term in a like manner when He said, "Wisdom is justified by all her children" (Luke 7:35). What did He mean? He certainly did not mean that wisdom is brought into a state of grace by having babies. He simply meant that the wisdom of various actions can be demonstrated by the fruit they bear.

So, James is addressing the demonstration or manifestation of true faith. When he says, "Was not Abraham our father justified by works when he offered up his son Isaac on the altar?" he is not saying that Abraham was brought into a state of grace by offering Isaac, but that he vindicated or demonstrated that his claim to faith was genuine.

Paul uses the term *justified* in the highest theological sense of a person being made just before God. He is dealing with justification in the sense of our ultimate reconciliation with the just and holy God. He wrote the epistle to the Romans largely to explain how salvation is accomplished, so he labors the point that justification is not by works of the law but by faith apart from works, that we are justified not by our own righteousness but by the righteousness of Christ. So, if we look carefully at these passages and think through the different questions that they are addressing, the difficulty evaporates.

Roman Catholic and Protestant affirmations

Rome, however, still refuses to drop its objections, and it continues to teach the same view of justification that was put forward by Trent. These statements from the Catechism of the Catholic Church (1995) touch on some of the matters we have discussed:

> Justification has been merited for us by the Passion of Christ who offered himself on the cross as a living victim, holy and pleasing to God, and whose blood has become the instrument of atonement for the sins of all men. Justification is conferred in Baptism, the sacrament of faith. It conforms us to the righteousness of God, who makes us inwardly just by the power of his mercy. Its purpose is the glory of God and of Christ, and the gift of eternal life. (Section 1992)

> The grace of Christ is the gratuitous gift that God makes to us of his own life, infused by the Holy Spirit into our soul to heal it of sin and to sanctify it. It is the sanctifying or deifying grace received in Baptism. It is in us the source of the work of sanctification. (1999)

> Justification has been merited for us by the Passion of Christ. It is granted us through Baptism. It conforms us to the righteousness of God, who justifies us. It has for its goal the glory of God and of Christ, and the gift of eternal life. It is the most excellent work of God's mercy. (2020)

We can therefore hope in the glory of heaven promised by God to those who love him and do his will. In every circumstance, each one of us should hope, with the grace of God, to persevere "to the end" and to obtain the joy of heaven, as God's eternal reward for the good works accomplished with the grace of Christ. In hope, the Church prays for "all men to be saved." She longs to be united with Christ, her Bridegroom, in the glory of heaven. (1821)

Over against these statements stand the clear, biblical affirmations of the Westminster Confession of Faith.

Those whom God effectually calleth, he also freely justifieth: not by infusing righteousness into them, but by pardoning their sins, and by accounting and accepting their persons as righteous; not for any thing wrought in them, or done by them, but for Christ's sake alone; not by imputing faith itself, the act of believing, or any other evangelical obedience to them, as their righteousness; but by imputing the obedience and satisfaction of Christ unto them, they receiving and resting on him and his righteousness by faith; which faith they have not of themselves, it is the gift of God. (11.1)

Faith, thus receiving and resting on Christ and his righteousness, is the alone instrument of justification; yet is it not alone in the person justified, but is ever accompanied with all other saving graces, and is no dead faith, but worketh by love. (11.2)

I have often told my seminary students that the doctrine of justification by faith alone is not all that hard to understand. It does not require a PhD in theology. Yet as simple as it is, it is one of the hardest truths of Scripture to get into the bloodstream. It is hard for us to understand that there is nothing we can do to earn, to deserve, or to add to the merit of Jesus Christ, and that when we stand before the judgment seat of God, we come with nothing in our hands. We must simply cling to the cross of Christ and put our trust in Him alone. Any church that teaches something other than this foundational truth has departed from the gospel.

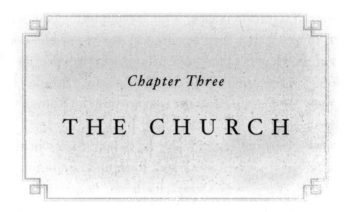

Chapter Three

THE CHURCH

MUCH COULD BE SAID ABOUT the Roman Catholic doctrine of the church, but I want to focus on the most important aspect of that doctrine, the relationship of the church to salvation. Rome has given mixed signals as to its true beliefs in this area, so I want to briefly review what it has said and then try to determine exactly where it stands in the twenty-first century.

The Roman Catholic Church is usually described as an institution that is sacerdotal, a term that comes from the Latin *sacerdos*, which means "priest." Sacerdotalism is a school of thought that teaches that salvation is mediated through the functions of the priesthood, namely, the sacraments. The great emphasis in Protestant churches is the preaching of the Word of God; this emphasis is even manifested in Protestant church architecture, with the pulpit being placed at the front and center, the focus of attention. However, in the Roman Catholic tradition, the center of attention is the altar. The Mass, the sacrament of the Eucharist, is seen as the heart of the liturgy rather than the sermon, which is usually a very short homily. The Eucharist must be conducted by a priest or bishop.

However, if salvation is sacerdotal, if redemption comes through the means of grace that are dispensed by the priest and controlled by the church, what happens to a person who is not a member of a sacerdotal communion such as the Roman Catholic Church? From Rome's perspective, can a person outside the Roman Catholic Church be saved?

This was a burning question in the United States in the 1940s and 1950s. When I was growing up in a suburban community outside Pittsburgh, there was a very clearly defined spirit of division between the Protestants and the Roman Catholics. It was manifested in the sociological division of the neighborhood; the Roman Catholics lived on one side of the main highway and the Protestants lived on the other side. The Protestants all went to the Protestant church and their children went to the public school; the Roman Catholics all went to the Roman Catholic Church and their children went to the Roman Catholic school. There was virtually no interchange socially between the two groups, and there was a severe element of distrust and suspicion between them.

However, when I went into the tenth grade, suddenly I and the other Protestant students were thrown together with the Roman Catholics, because the Roman Catholics at that point did not have their own high school. Suddenly, football and baseball teams were made up of a mixture of Protestants and Roman Catholics, and there were some beginnings of communication and friendship.

However, one Roman Catholic acquaintance told me he had been taught in his Roman Catholic parochial school that anyone who was a Protestant could not go to heaven, because a person had to be within the Roman Catholic Church in order to be saved. Later, I developed a very close friendship with a man who was a Roman Catholic, and when I was about to be married to Vesta, I wanted him to be my best man at the wedding. He had to ask for special permission from the church to participate in my Protestant wedding, but it was refused on the grounds that it was considered to be a serious sin to even attend a Protestant worship service. So, my best friend was not even allowed to attend my wedding, let alone participate in it. When he got married later, I was given permission by the bishop of New York to participate in his wedding, but I was not permitted to approach the altar for the time of the consummation of the vows in the marriage Mass.

When I went to seminary, I served as a student minister in a small Hungarian refugee church in a depressed community. In that community, there were eight Roman Catholic churches and one tiny Protestant church. I moved into the small manse next door to the church in the fall. During Halloween, the manse was the favorite target of the children of the community. Mud and tomatoes were thrown at the house, and garbage was left on the lawn. I found out later that all this was done by children from the community, but they were children I did not know and with whom I had had no contact. However, when I managed to question some of these children, I discovered that their parents had told them that the Devil lived in the manse. It turned out that it was a regular practice during Halloween to bombard the bastion of Protestantism.

I share these illustrations only to show that this kind of attitude did not vanish hundreds of years ago. In my lifetime, I experienced strong suspicions simply because I was Protestant. Thankfully, this kind of suspicion is foreign in American culture today. The changes enacted by Vatican Council II have produced a very different atmosphere. But where did this suspicion come from in the first place? What was the theological and historical basis for this kind of attitude?

Cyprian and Augustine

Cyprian (d. 258), an early church father and the bishop of Carthage, developed a formula that has been very important in the development of the Roman Catholic understanding of the relationship of the church to salvation. The classic phrase or formula given by Cyprian is the statement, *"Extra ecclesiam nulla salus."* Let me explain what this statement means. *Extra* means "outside of" or "apart from." *Ecclesiam* means "the church." *Nulla* means "none" or "no." Finally, *salus* means "salvation." So, Cyprian said, "Outside of the church, no salvation." He went on to formulate an analogy that likened the church to Noah's ark. He said it is just as necessary for a person to be concretely, really, and visibly within the membership of the Roman Catholic Church in order to be saved as it was necessary for a person to be concretely, really, and visibly within the ark of Noah in order to be rescued from the flood. No person could be said to be with Noah in spirit and survive the flood if he literally missed the boat. He had to be in that ark, not outside looking in.

This notion was modified to some degree by the great Augustine (354–430), who is considered the supreme theologian of the church in terms of Roman Catholic ecclesiology. Augustine had a very strong view of the church, and he, more than any theologian of the first millennium, developed and articulated a systematic doctrine of the church. His famous statement is often repeated in Roman circles: "He who does not have the church as his mother does not have God as his Father." This statement is the root of the idea of "holy mother church," in whose bosom one must safely abide in order to be redeemed.

However, Augustine's ecclesiology introduced some very sophisticated notions that counteracted a crass Cyprianic view. These ideas were driven by the Donatist controversy of the fourth century. This controversy focused on the legitimacy of *lapsi* priests. The notion of the *lapsi* had its origins even earlier, in the days of the persecutions that were ordered by the Emperor Diocletian (reigned 284–305) in the fourth century, when people were called to recant their faith in Christ. Church history gives us the triumphant record of multitudes of faithful Christians who boldly professed their faith in Christ in the face of threats of persecution and death. These men and women are remembered as the martyrs of the church. But not everyone who was called upon to bear the witness of martyrdom acted so heroically. There were those, including some priests and bishops, who broke under the pressure and repudiated their faith in Christ. When the fires of persecution died away, the question of how to treat those who had lapsed from the faith came to the fore. Could they be restored? Was their liturgical function, their priestly service, valid or invalid?

There was a wing in the church, the so-called Donatists, who insisted on a strict Cyprianic understanding of the church. They maintained that the visible church is the true church only when its leaders are spiritually pure. They said that the sacraments were not valid if they were administered by a priest who had lapsed, was heretical, or was living in mortal sin. The corruption of those doing the administration made the sacraments invalid.

What kinds of problems did this understanding raise for people in the church? When Vesta and I were making preparations for our marriage, we wanted the wedding ceremony to be especially holy and sacred. We had both been raised and confirmed in the same church, so there was no question as to where we were going to be married. It was the church of our families, the church of our heritage. Yet, when Vesta and I were converted to Christianity, the pastor of the church ridiculed our conversions, and he told me straightforwardly that if I believed in the physical resurrection of Christ, I was "a damned fool." When a man repudiates the resurrection of Christ, I have serious questions about his Christian commitment. I do not consider the doctrine of the resurrection of Christ to be a subject for intramural debate among different persuasions of theology; I consider it to be an essential aspect of Christian faith. But this man had denied it clearly and directly in my presence. So, I had questions about the man's faith, and even though I was not in seminary yet, I wondered whether his lack of belief would make the marriage ceremony invalid. If my pastor was, in fact, an unbeliever, and if the Donatists were right, that all the liturgical actions of an unbeliever or heretic are invalidated by his corruption, my marriage would not be valid. This is the kind of problem believers in the fourth century faced.

This raging controversy drove Augustine to develop his four classic marks of the church. He said the church is one, holy, catholic (or "universal"), and Apostolic. It was the second item, the holiness of the church, that was at the center of the Donatist controversy, although universality was also involved. Augustine said that the church is holy because of its unity with Christ and because of the activity of the Holy Spirit within it. That is to say, he did not maintain that the church is intrinsically holy, independently holy, but its holiness is derived, dependent, and contingent. He was quick to point out that this does not mean that everyone within the church is holy, but they are in the place where the holiness of God is focused. He acknowledged that there are tares along with the wheat, who, though they are in the presence of holiness, remain more or less untouched by it. He went on to say that the visible church has the means of grace by which holiness comes. However, not everyone makes diligent use of the means of grace. Further, he maintained that the church will be without spot or wrinkle only in heaven, and to expect the church to be pure in order for its work to be valid is an exercise in futility. He saw in the Donatists a premature longing for what is promised only for the future, in the heavenly church. He declared that if, as the Donatists said, the church had to be morally and spiritually perfect in order for it to be a true church, not even the Donatist churches were true churches. There could be no true churches in the world, because no churches are perfect.

Augustine spoke of the church as a *corpus per mixtum*, "a mixed body," that is, a mix of true believers and unbelievers. Nevertheless, he said, the people of God, the company of the elect, exist substantially within the visible church, though he admitted that there might be some outside the church who are believers. So, Augustine modified the strong view of visible membership as an essential ingredient for salvation. He cracked open the door to the possibility of redemption for those who are not visibly, physically united with the church (though, of course, they should be).

Invincible ignorance

The Council of Florence (1431–45) restated the necessity of being within the visible church in order to experience salvation. This council declared: "All those who are outside the catholic church, not only pagans but also Jews or heretics and schismatics, cannot share in eternal life and will go into the everlasting fire which was prepared for the devil and his angels, unless they are joined to the catholic church before the end of their lives."[1]

In the years after the Reformation, this problem became more difficult for Rome. Within a generation or two, the grandchildren of the original Reformers were filling Lutheran, Anglican and Reformed churches all over Europe. Entire nations declared themselves Protestant, leaving no Roman Catholic witness in these areas. The Protestants still worshiped God in Christ, still held to the major truths of the Bible and the earliest ecumenical councils, and still sought to be obedient disciples. Were they to be placed in the same category as their forefathers (the Reformers), who knowingly and willfully said "No" to holy mother church?

One pope in modern times has distinguished himself as the chief papal barrier to reconciliation between Rome and the Reformation—Pius IX, who served from 1846 to 1878. However, he also brought moderation to the hard line of the ancient Cyprianic view. In 1863, in a very significant encyclical titled *Quanto Conficiamur Moerore* ("On Promotion of False Doctrines"), Pius maintained the seriousness of being outside the visible institution of Rome. Nevertheless, he gave an important new qualifier, speaking of a kind of provision of grace or indulgence for those who suffer from what he called "invincible ignorance." He wrote:

> It is again necessary to mention and censure a very grave error entrapping some Catholics who believe that it is possible to arrive at eternal salvation although living in error and alienated from the true faith and Catholic unity. Such belief is certainly opposed to Catholic teaching. There are, of course, those who are struggling with invincible ignorance about our most holy religion. Sincerely observing the natural law and its precepts inscribed by God on all hearts and ready to obey God, they live honest lives and are able to attain eternal life by the efficacious virtue of divine light and grace. Because God knows, searches and clearly understands the minds, hearts, thoughts, and nature of all, his supreme kindness and clemency do not permit anyone at all who is not guilty of deliberate sin to suffer eternal punishments.[2]

Invincible ignorance is an important concept in Roman Catholic theology, particularly with respect to the relationship of Protestants to the Roman community. Invincible ignorance is ignorance that cannot be overcome, therefore providing an excuse (as distinguished from vincible ignorance, which can be and should be conquered, and therefore provides no excuse). In Romans 1:20, Paul says men are "without excuse" because God's general revelation of Himself is so clear. At judgment day, no one will be able to claim to have no knowledge of God and plead invincible ignorance. They may plead ignorance, but it will be vincible ignorance, which will render them inexcusable.

Suppose you are driving through a city and approach a stoplight. The light for your lane is red, but you proceed past it without stopping. Next you notice a blue light on the roof of a car behind you. When the police officer approaches your vehicle and informs you that you have earned a ticket for failing to stop at a red light, you say: "I'm sorry, officer, I didn't mean to do anything wrong. I didn't know that it was against the law to drive my car through a red light in this city. You see, I don't live here. I'm from another city." The officer would say, "I'm sorry, but ignorance of the law is no excuse." When you drive, no matter where you might be, you are responsible and liable for knowledge of the highway laws in that location. Such laws are not hidden; they are readily available. Thus, your ignorance could have been overcome. So, it does not excuse you.

But suppose the city planners are trying to balance the budget, so they secretly decide that as of 9 a.m. the next day all vehicles will be required to stop on green lights and proceed on red lights. Violations of this new law will be met with hefty fines. Then they notify the police force about the change, but they tell no one else. The law is enacted in secret. Therefore, no driver has any way of knowing about it. So, if you drive into the city after 9 a.m. the next day, drive through a green light, and receive a ticket, you can appeal the fine on the basis of invincible ignorance. You had an excuse—you were not told that the law was changed.

This was the kind of crack in the door that Pius IX gave to Protestants who had been born and raised in Protestant communities, and therefore never exposed to Roman Catholic teaching and the truth of Roman Catholicism. These people conceivably could be Roman Catholics had they been exposed to the truth. Since they were not, they are granted the indulgence of invincible ignorance.

This is not a blanket indulgence for all Protestants. Pius IX distinguished between those who are genuinely invincibly ignorant and those who are stiff-necked offenders who know the truth but refuse to submit to it. Those people have no hope of salvation. He wrote, "Eternal salvation cannot be obtained by those who oppose the authority and statements of the same Church and are stubbornly separated from the unity of the Church and also from the successor of Peter, the Roman Pontiff."[3]

Additional strong warnings regarding the necessity and urgency of being members of the Roman Catholic Church were given in 1943 in Pope Pius XII's encyclical *Mystici Corporis Christi* ("The Mystical Body of Christ"), in which he identified the visible Roman Catholic Church with the mystical body of Christ. This meant that anyone outside the visible Roman church was outside the body of Christ. So, once again the church took a hard line.

Desire for the church

I mentioned in the introduction that Vatican I referred to Protestants as schismatics and heretics, but Vatican II referred to them as "separated brethren." This alteration in language represented a new attitude, particularly in the West, among Roman Catholics toward Protestants, a tremendous shift from Vatican I.

Vatican II, like many of the great councils of the church that have been held through the centuries, was called an "ecumenical council." This term comes from the Greek word *oikoumene*, which means "the inhabited world." Thus, an ecumenical council is a council of the worldwide Church of Rome; it is not restricted to the bishops of a city, a country, or a continent, but all nations are represented. Roman Catholics recognize twenty-one councils from church history as ecumenical, while Protestants generally recognize the first several ecumenical councils, held from the fourth to ninth centuries. Obviously, since the Reformation, all "ecumenical" councils have been strictly Roman Catholic gatherings. At Vatican II, for instance, Protestants were allowed to attend as observers, but they were not given voting rights.

The use of the term "ecumenical council" for Vatican II created confusion. It was held in the 1960s, during the ecumenical movement, a push for greater unity among Protestant denominations. When Pope John XXIII called Vatican Council II and spoke of it as an ecumenical council, many Protestants took that to mean that Rome was interested in participating actively in the ecumenical movement, that Rome was putting out overtures of union and reunification with the "separated brethren."

Of course, Vatican II was not an overt act of reconciliation with Protestantism. However, there was a genuine spirit of openness in Vatican II that was unprecedented in Roman Catholic history. Voices were outspoken at the council against the spirit of triumphalism that was implied by the old Cyprianic line. The accent was placed on the church's function as servant rather than as lord, on its ministry of shepherding rather than of dominion.

Out of that atmosphere came a new discussion of the place of Protestants *vis a vis* the Roman Catholic Church. There arose a new concept in the Roman Catholic Church, the idea of the *votum ecclesiae*, or "the desire to belong to the church."

The *votum ecclesiae* has its roots in the importance of baptism in Roman Catholic theology. When we examine the Roman view of the sacraments, we will see that baptism is believed to operate *ex opere operato*, that is, "by the working of the works," automatically giving justifying grace to those who receive it. If one does not have baptism, he is in a serious position. This is why, even to this day, nurses in the delivery rooms of hospitals are authorized to administer emergency baptisms in the case of dying Roman Catholic infants, to make sure that those infants do not die unbaptized. Baptism is the instrumental cause of justification.

However, some Roman Catholic scholars raised the scenario of a person who professes faith and states that he wants to unite with the Roman Catholic Church, but who dies before he is baptized. Is that person therefore condemned because he does not receive baptism so as to be justified? The Roman Catholic Church has a provision known as the *votum baptismi*, or "the desire of baptism." If a person desires baptism but is hindered from receiving it by providential circumstances, in the eyes of the church he is considered baptized. He does not have the actual rite, but he has the spiritual grace because he has a true and authentic desire for baptism. So, building on that idea, some Roman scholars suggested that Protestants could be considered members of the Roman Catholic Church by means of a *votum ecclesiae*, a desire for the church.

Roman Catholic theology is noted for making fine distinctions, and the *votum ecclesiae* is no exception. The *votum ecclesiae explicitum* is an *explicit* desire to unite with Rome. This category covers the person who is in similar circumstances to the man who dies before receiving baptism. It has to do with a person outside Rome, a Protestant, who learns of the Roman Catholic Church, hears Roman teaching and believes it, and desires to join the church. He goes through the whole catechetical process and is actually on his way to join the church, to physically and visibly enter the ark, as it were, but dies in a traffic accident before he arrives. He had an explicit, stated desire to join the church, but he never actually consummated that desire. Such a person is considered a member of the Roman Catholic Church.

The broader category is the *votum ecclesiae implicitum*, which is an *implicit* desire to join the Roman Catholic Church. In this category is the person who has been "brainwashed" by Protestant ministers who preach and teach against Rome, and has actually become convinced by these faulty arguments and duped into accepting heretical views. But in his heart of hearts, he has a genuine desire to be in the true church; he just does not know where it is. This takes us back to the idea of invincible ignorance. If he only knew the truth, he would not obstinately refuse to submit to it. He would move heaven and earth to become a member of the Roman Catholic Church. Since there remains in his heart the slight desire to be truly obedient to God and to Christ, he can be considered a member of the Roman Catholic Church by means of the *votum ecclesiae implicitum*. There is no need for an expressed desire to actually join the church. He only needs to have an inward desire to please God, which by implication is a desire to be in the true church, which by implication is Rome. Obviously, this is an extremely broad qualification, far different from Cyprian's analogy of the ark.

Rome's acceptance of the Cyprianic formula has changed so radically, a Boston priest, Father Leonard Feeney, was excommunicated in 1953 for teaching the hard-line view that there is no salvation outside the Roman Catholic church. Furthermore, Pope Paul VI, in a 1965 decree, wrote that priests "are to live as good shepherds that know their sheep, and they are to seek to lead those who are not of this sheepfold that they, too, may hear the voice of Christ, so that there might be one fold and one shepherd,"[4] implying that there are actual sheep outside the sheepfold, the Roman Catholic Church. Finally, Rome sometimes speaks of *vestigia ecclesiae*, or "traces of the church," that can be found in other communions. According to this concept, there are vestigial remnants of the true church still functioning in other churches. Even though there are no other true churches as such, for only the Roman Catholic Church is the mystical body of Christ, still there is truth and grace in other churches, and people are truly saved there.

Roman Catholic and Protestant affirmations

So, there is no doubt that in some respects, the Roman Catholic Church seems to have softened its stance that it alone is the one true church. However, at other times it seems to reassert that idea. In the Catechism of the Catholic Church (1995), Rome states, regarding the affirmation that "outside the church there is no salvation":

How are we to understand this affirmation, often repeated by the Church Fathers? Re-formulated positively, it means that all salvation comes from Christ the Head through the Church which is his Body: "Basing itself on Scripture and Tradition, the Council teaches that the Church, a pilgrim now on earth, is necessary for salvation: the one Christ is the mediator and the way of salvation; he is present to us in his body which is the Church. He himself explicitly asserted the necessity of faith and Baptism, and thereby affirmed at the same time the necessity of the Church which men enter through Baptism as through a door. Hence they could not be saved who, knowing that the Catholic Church was founded as necessary by God through Christ, would refuse either to enter it or to remain in it" (Vatican II, *Lumen Gentium*, 14). (Section 846)

But this affirmation is followed immediately by a softening clause:

This affirmation is not aimed at those who, through no fault of their own, do not know Christ and his Church: "Those who, through no fault of their own, do not know the Gospel of Christ or his Church, but who nevertheless seek God with a sincere heart, and, moved by grace, try in their actions to do his will as they know it through the dictates of their conscience—those too may achieve eternal salvation" (Vatican II, *Lumen Gentium*, 16). (847)

Finally, in 2007, the Roman Catholic Church, with the approval of Pope Benedict XVI, released a document titled "Responses to Some Questions Regarding Certain Aspects of the Doctrine on the Church." It states: "According to Catholic doctrine, these Communities do not enjoy apostolic succession in the sacrament of

Orders, and are, therefore, deprived of a constitutive element of the Church. These ecclesial Communities which, specifically because of the absence of the sacramental priesthood, have not preserved the genuine and integral substance of the Eucharistic Mystery cannot, according to Catholic doctrine, be called "Churches" in the proper sense."[5] This document sparked a firestorm of criticism, as it seemed to reassert the old Cyprian formula that there is only one true church.

Over against these Roman Catholic teachings, note the balance and fairness of the Westminster Confession of Faith:

The catholic or universal Church, which is invisible, consists of the whole number of the elect, that have been, are, or shall be gathered into one, under Christ the head thereof; and is the spouse, the body, the fullness of Him that filleth all in all. (25.1)

The visible Church, which is also catholic or universal under the Gospel (not confined to one nation, as before under the law), consists of all those throughout the world that profess the true religion; and of their children: and is the kingdom of the Lord Jesus Christ, the house and family of God, out of which there is no ordinary possibility of salvation. (25.2)

Unto this catholic and visible Church, Christ hath given the ministry, oracles, and ordinances of God, for the gathering and perfecting of the saints, in this life, to the end of the world; and doth by his own presence and Spirit, according to his promise, make them effectual thereunto. (25.3)

This catholic Church hath been sometimes more, sometimes less, visible. And particular Churches, which are members thereof, are more or less pure, according as the doctrine of the gospel is taught and embraced, ordinances administered, and public worship performed more or less purely in them. (25.4)

The purest Churches under heaven are subject both to mixture and error: and some have so degenerated as to become apparently no Churches of Christ. Nevertheless, there shall be always a Church on earth, to worship God according to his will. (25.5)

I believe Rome needs to clarify where it stands on this issue definitively. This is very important for Rome to work out given that it is a sacerdotal institution. If justification is not by faith or trust in Christ alone, but occurs primarily by means of the sacraments, most importantly the sacraments of baptism and penance, which require the function of the priest to perform, then Protestant churches cannot provide salvation, and Rome must be the only true church. But if Protestants are correct in their doctrine of justification, Rome is not a true church at all. Rome cannot have it both ways.

Chapter Four

THE
SACRAMENTS

IN RECENT YEARS, IN CERTAIN quarters of the Protestant church, there has been a renewed interest in liturgy and the nature of sacramental religion. This revival of interest in the sacraments comes at a time when the world is becoming more and more devoted to secularism. The sacred and sacramental are being restored in some circles as an answer to this drift toward deeper secularism.

The Roman Catholic Church, however, has always had a strong view of the sacramental character of life. One of the reasons the Roman Church has seven sacraments, rather than two as in most Protestant communions, is that a fundamental sacramental approach to man underlies Rome's theology. So, this is an important area of difference and disagreement between Protestants and Roman Catholics. I must note that it is not easy to compare the monolithic Roman Catholic position to the highly varying Protestant positions. Protestant communities do not always agree on the nature, function, and significance of the various sacraments. In fact, during the Reformation, the Reformed churches found it impossible to achieve unity with the Lutheran churches because of differences over their understanding of the Lord's Supper. Protestant differences on the sacraments are not new.

The basic differences have to do with the number of sacraments, the nature of the sacraments, the efficacy of the sacraments (that is, in terms of what the sacraments do, what they accomplish, their function, and so forth), and the mode of the sacraments. That fourth point may be the most significant of them all, because the Roman Catholic Church believes the sacraments do what they are designed to do *ex opere operato*, that is, "by the working of the works." In other words, simply performing the sacrament causes it to operate and perform what it is designed to perform. According to this view, the sacraments automatically convey grace to the recipient. So, in this chapter I will briefly survey the seven rites that are regarded as sacraments in the Roman Catholic Church, touching on how they are understood and what they are thought to accomplish. I will conclude with a brief look at the Protestant position.

The Roman Catholic sacraments

The English word *sacrament* comes from the Latin word *sacramentum*, which is the equivalent of the Greek word *mysterion*. Of course, we get the English word *mystery* from the Greek *mysterion*. Oddly, the term *mysterion* in the New Testament never has reference to what we call sacraments. It has an entirely different meaning, but in contemporary speech we use *mystery* in a broader sense to refer to the hidden, mystical, transcendent dimension of the sacraments. This is why the Roman Catholic Church speaks of the sacraments as "holy mysteries."

Historically, the Roman church has identified seven ecclesiastical rites as sacraments. The number of seven sacraments was fixed by Rome at the Second Council of Lyon (1274), at the Council of Florence (1431–45), and at the Council of Trent (1545–63). So, as early as the thirteenth century, the Roman Catholic Church had fixed the number of sacraments at seven.

The rationale for the different sacraments and the selection of
seven was seen as analogous to the medieval concept of the seven
stages of life. Thus, there is sacramental grace for people at every stage
of their lives. The sacrament for the initial stage of life is baptism.
As a person makes the transition from childhood to young adult-
hood, there is confirmation. When he enters marriage, there is the
sacrament of matrimony. At the conclusion of life, there is extreme
unction. In addition, three special graces offer divine assistance for
living in the world. The sacrament of holy orders, or ordination, is
for those who are entering into a special ministry of the church,
people who are instruments of God to assist others. Then there are
two sacraments that are believed to give the most assistance in this
world. One is penance, which gives assistance for the whole life after
baptism. The other is the sacrament of the Lord's Supper, which is
seen as the sacrament that is above all others in the Roman Catholic
Church. Some have spoken of these seven sacraments in terms of
the four dimensions of earth and the three dimensions of heaven,
but that idea is not part of the official teaching of the church.

Baptism

The sacrament of baptism is the first sacrament that is administered
to a person in the Roman Catholic Church. As I mentioned above,
Rome holds that baptism conveys grace *ex opere operato*, and the grace
that is conveyed by baptism is the grace of regeneration. This means
that when a person is baptized, he is born again of the Spirit and
the disposition of his soul is changed, leaving him justified in the
sight of God. As I have noted previously, righteousness is "infused"
or poured into his soul. Rome, then, believes and teaches that the
prerequisite for justification, the instrumental cause, is baptism. In
Protestant theology, by contrast, the instrumental cause is faith, and
God "imputes" righteousness to the believer.

However, even though baptism cleanses a person of the power

and guilt of original sin and infuses into him the grace of justification, it does not leave him perfectly sanctified. There is still something of the nature of sin left over. In Roman terms, baptism leaves a person with concupiscence, an inclination or disposition toward sin, which accounts for the fact that baptized people frequently fall back into sin. However, concupiscence is not itself sin. This is a point of disagreement for Protestants, for whom anything that is a disposition to sin *is* sin.

According to Rome, sins that are committed after baptism, especially mortal sins, destroy the justifying grace of baptism, which makes it necessary for a person to be justified again. Mortal sins are called "mortal" because they have the power and capacity to destroy the grace of justification that comes in baptism. The sacrament of penance, which we will consider below, is designed to solve this problem.

Confirmation

Following baptism, Roman Catholics receive the sacrament of confirmation. Rome does not regard confirmation as a new infusion of grace in addition to baptism, but as an increase of grace unto maturity. In other words, confirmation strengthens, undergirds, and moves the grace that is given in baptism toward maturity. If I may use a crass analogy, it is a kind of "booster shot."

Confirmation is distinguished from baptism as a separate rite, but it presupposes baptism. Confirmation cannot happen apart from baptism. In fact, the word *confirmation* itself suggests that that which was done earlier is now being firmed up, as it were.

In most cases, confirmation is administered when a child reaches the "age of discretion," the age when he can understand the rite (usually taken to be around the age of seven). It is usually administered by a bishop and involves anointing with oil and the laying on of hands.

Matrimony

The sacrament of matrimony, like baptism, involves an infusion of grace. The special grace of marriage is given by God to strengthen the union of a man and a woman. Thus, a wedding is not merely an external rite involving promises, sanctions, and authoritative decrees, but special grace is given to the couple to enable them to accomplish a real mystical union.

Extreme unction

The sacrament of extreme unction is based on an exhortation in the book of James: "Is anyone among you sick? Let him call for the elders of the church, and let them pray over him, anointing him with oil in the name of the Lord. And the prayer of faith will save the one who is sick, and the Lord will raise him up. And if he has committed sins, he will be forgiven" (5:14–15). Originally, extreme unction was a healing rite, not a last rite, and the Roman Catholic Church only recently reemphasized that it is a gift of grace that is to be used any time a person is seriously ill, not with a view simply to prepare him for death, but hopefully to bring healing. Its primary use, however, is as a final anointing of grace to strengthen penance, lest a person die with mortal sin in his life and therefore go to hell, the mortal sin having killed the grace of justification.

Extreme unction is administered to people whose lives are thought to be in danger due to illness or old age. It is administered by a priest, who applies oil that has been consecrated and blessed by a bishop to the forehead (usually in the shape of a cross) and to the hands while praying.

Holy orders

The sacrament of holy orders is the ordination of a priest, bishop, or deacon. It also gives an infusion of grace, which confers special powers to those who receive it. The two special powers given to a priest in ordination are the power of absolution and the power of consecration. Absolution is the power to forgive sins as part of the sacrament of penance, allowing the recipient to receive the sacraments without sin. Consecration is the act by which the bread and wine used in the Lord's Supper are set apart and, according to Roman Catholic belief, transformed into the body and blood of Christ. The priest accomplishes the act of consecration by speaking the words of institution.

When Martin Luther was ordained as a priest and was called upon to officiate at his first Mass, at the moment in the liturgy for the consecration of the elements, he froze with fear and was unable to continue. He was terrified and awestruck by the enormity of the power that had been placed upon him, the power to speak words by which the normal elements of bread and wine are transformed substantially into the body and blood of Christ.

The two sacraments that are most significant in the Roman Catholic Church and most divisive in terms of Rome's relations with Protestantism are penance and the Lord's Supper, or the Eucharist. Most people believe that the big difference between the Roman Catholic Church and the Protestant churches is the fact that Rome has seven sacraments and Protestants have only two. But the real difference is focused in these two sacraments and the way in which they are understood. Therefore, I want to give more extensive consideration to penance and the Lord's Supper than I have given to the other five Roman Catholic sacraments.

Penance

The sacrament of penance is crucial to the division between Protestantism and Roman Catholicism because it touches on the two central issues of the debate between the Reformers and Rome—the issue of justification specifically and the broader issue of merit and grace. This is the eye of the hurricane; these are the real issues that divide Rome from Protestants.

As I mentioned in chapter 2, when Martin Luther responded to the *Diatribe* of Desiderius Erasmus in the sixteenth century, he actually thanked Erasmus for not bothering him with trifling matters. He was pleased that Erasmus had not focused on questions such as the authority of the pope, the function of Mary, the liturgical rites of the church, or relics. Those matters are important; in fact, we are dealing with some of them in this book. However, Luther perceived that Erasmus was dealing with the doctrine of justification by faith alone, which, in Luther's view, was the article upon which the church stands or falls. Other matters could be debated, but the question of how a person is justified has eternal consequences.

The sacrament of penance was instituted by the church to help people who commit mortal sin. As I mentioned in the introduction, it is regarded as the second plank of justification for those who have made shipwreck of their souls.[1] One makes shipwreck of his soul by committing mortal sin, which destroys the grace of justification. However, the person can be restored to justification through penance.

The form of the sacrament of penance is absolution, wherein the priest says, "*Te absolvo*," which means, "I absolve you." This practice has been very repugnant to Protestants. If you were to ask a group of Protestants to identify their main disagreements with Roman Catholicism, you almost certainly would hear one of them say, "I don't have to confess my sins to a priest; I can pray by myself." Protestants tend to become very indignant about required confession. If you probe further, one of them is likely to ask who the priest thinks he is to say "*Te absolvo*." Protestants are zealous to insist that forgiveness comes from Christ, not from a mere man, even if he is a priest. But the issue between Protestantism and Roman Catholicism is not confession or absolution. In fact, many Protestant church services include corporate confession of sin followed by an assurance of pardon, wherein the minister shares a biblical promise, such as 1 John 1:9: "If we confess our sins, he is faithful and just to forgive us our sins and to cleanse us from all unrighteousness." That is absolution. Also, Rome has been faithful to point out that when the priest says "*Te absolvo*," he is not presuming to say that he has the authority or the power in and of himself to absolve anyone, but he is speaking in the name of Jesus Christ and in the name of the church, to whom the Lord gave the authority to bind and loose (Matt. 16:19; 18:18). So, there is really no great debate between Protestants and Roman Catholics about the idea of confessing sins.

There are three dimensions to the sacrament of penance—contrition, confession, and satisfaction. Contrition means turning away from sin out of a genuine sense of having offended God, a brokenness of heart, not merely a fear of punishment, which we call attrition. The Roman Catholic prayer of contrition is as follows: "O my God, I am heartily sorry for having offended Thee, and I detest all my sins because I dread the loss of heaven and the pains of hell; but most of all because they offend Thee, my God, who art all-good and deserving of all my love. I firmly resolve, with the help of Thy grace, to confess my sins, to do penance, and to amend my life. Amen." Much of that prayer, especially the parts about dreading the loss of heaven and the pains of hell, is attrition. But when the sinner expresses sorrow for having offended God, that is contrition.

The second dimension, confession, is, of course, the act of confessing one's sins. Protestants have no issue with contrition and confession. The issue is the third dimension of penance, which is satisfaction. Roman Catholics teach that for the sacrament to be complete, it is necessary for the penitent believer to do "works of satisfaction," which satisfy the demands of God's justice. So, a sinner is not off the hook when he confesses his sins; he still must do works of satisfaction. These works may be very small. The sinner may be required to say five "Hail Marys" or three "Our Fathers" (the "Hail

Mary" is a Roman Catholic prayer asking for the intercession of the Virgin Mary; the "Our Father" is the Lord's Prayer). But if his sins are especially severe, he may be required to make a pilgrimage. One of the favorite methods of doing works of satisfaction in the church historically has been the giving of alms.

As I noted earlier, Rome teaches that a work of satisfaction gives the penitent sinner congruous merit. This kind of merit is distinguished from condign merit. Condign merit is so meritorious that God must reward it; congruous merit is only so meritorious that it is congruous or fitting for God to reward it. Still, it is true merit. It is accrued to the person, and without that merit the penitent sinner, no matter how much faith and trust he has in the atonement of Jesus Christ, cannot be justified. So, he must do works of satisfaction in order to gain merit.

The Reformation debate on justification grew out of a practice that was inseparably related to the sacrament of penance, specifically to works of satisfaction and almsgiving. Almost any time a great theological controversy occurs in the church, it begins as a debate about some practice in the church. Usually, the debate over the practice itself gives way to a debate about the theological implications of the practice. In the case of the Reformation, that practice was the sale of indulgences.

What is an indulgence? Basically, an indulgence is a transfer of merit. In order to gain heaven, a person must have sufficient merit. If a person dies lacking in sufficient merit to go directly to heaven, he goes to purgatory, the purging place. Purgatory is not hell; it is the place where a person receives loving and sanctifying chastisement. By this chastisement, the person is made righteous enough to enter heaven; in other words, he accrues enough merit to get into heaven. A person might spend five minutes in purgatory or he might spend thousands of years there, depending on the deficiency of merit with which he enters purgatory.

However, the Roman Catholic Church came to believe it had the power to give merit to those who lacked it, in order to shorten their time in purgatory. Where did the church get this merit? It was said to come from works of supererogation, works that are more meritorious than God requires, such as a martyr's death or a sacrificial life. These works are performed by the saints, and the excess merits from these works form a treasury of merit that the church may tap in order to give an indulgence to a needy person in purgatory.

I believe that there is no concept within the Roman Catholic Church that is more basely repugnant to Protestants than the concept of the treasury of merit. A person who believes in justification by faith alone weeps at this notion. This is because Protestants also believe in a treasury of merit, one that is infinite and inexhaustible, but we believe that treasury is filled with the merit of the Son of God alone. The issue in the indulgences controversy is the sufficiency of Christ alone to redeem a person. According to Protestantism, justification happens on the basis of Christ's merit credited to His people. For Rome, we are never finally saved until we have sufficient merit of our own.

As I mentioned above, the practice of indulgences was a major contributing factor to the Reformation. Early in the sixteenth century, the Roman Church began making plans to rebuild St. Peter's Basilica in Rome. In 1517, Pope Leo X offered indulgences for those who gave alms for the basilica project. The church made it very clear that indulgences were not to be sold as if the church were conducting a crass funding drive. The church believed it was offering the faithful an alternative form of almsgiving as part of their works of satisfaction. So, no one was to give alms for the building of St. Peter's except out of a broken and contrite heart for his sins. In other words, the giving of these alms was to be inseparably related to the sacrament of penance, even though those giving the alms would receive special indulgences.

However, Johann Tetzel, a German Dominican preacher, began

selling indulgences. He did not call people to practice the sacrament of penance. He clearly was guilty of distorting the Roman Catholic system of indulgences, and Rome acknowledges that to this day. But Luther challenged Tetzel on his sale of indulgences, calling attention to it. His protest sparked a thorough examination of the merit system in light of the doctrine of justification by faith.

The Lord's Supper

In the sacrament of the Lord's Supper, according to the Roman Catholic Church, we have the miracle of the Mass, which is known as transubstantiation. The prefix *trans-* means "across," and *substantiation* derives from the word *substance*. So, transubstantiation involves a substance being carried or moved across.

The concept of substance, as defined in the Roman Catholic Church, borrows from the philosophical terminology of the ancient Greek philosopher Aristotle, who distinguished the substance and the accidens of an object. The substance is the essence of a thing, and the accidens are the external, perceivable qualities of that object, its outward appearances. If I look at a chair, I cannot see the essence of it, the atoms or the molecules, because they are too small for me to perceive them with my naked eye. But I can see the color, the shape, the texture, and other external qualities of the chair.

In the Eucharist, there is bread and wine. The substance of bread and wine and the accidens of bread and wine are present. According to Rome, in the miracle of the Mass, at the prayer of consecration, the substance of the elements is transformed supernaturally into the substance of the body and blood of Christ, but the accidens of bread and wine remain. The bread still looks like bread, tastes like bread, feels like bread, and smells like bread. If the priest drops it on the floor, it makes a sound like a piece of bread hitting the floor. But it is not bread. The substance of it, the essence of it, has been supernaturally transformed to the body, the flesh, of Jesus Christ. Likewise, the substance of the wine has been transformed to the substance of the blood of Christ.

Why do Roman Catholics, when they go into the church, genuflect, or kneel, before sitting down? Why does the priest genuflect so often when he's moving around at the altar? On the altar of every Roman Catholic church there is a holy vessel called the tabernacle. Sometimes it is a simple square box, but sometimes it is more ornate. That is the focal point of all the genuflection. People kneel in veneration and adoration because of the presence of the tabernacle. But it is not the box that people are acknowledging; it is what is inside the box. The tabernacle contains the consecrated host, the bread and wine that have been transformed into the body and blood of Christ. Roman Catholics are convinced that the real body and blood of Christ are in that box. He is there substantially, physically.

The celebration of the Mass is described in the Catechism of the Catholic Church as "the Holy Sacrifice." That has prompted Protestants to argue that if the bread is really the body of Christ and the priest breaks it, the church is ripping and tearing the body of Christ again when the Scriptures tell us that He was broken for us once and for all, that He was the final, full, sufficient sacrifice for the sin of His people (Heb. 7:27; 10:12–14). Is not Christ's body being mutilated again in the Mass? Are we not inflicting torment on the One who has finished His work of sacrifice? Rome nuances its teaching on the sacrificial aspect of the Mass, saying that it is an unbloody sacrifice and that it makes present the one sacrifice of Christ. However, the whole idea of any kind of sacrifice happening in new-covenant worship is repugnant to Protestants, who hold that the value, the significance, and the merit of Christ's suffering on the cross was so great that to repeat it is to denigrate it.

Protestants also struggle with the question of how the human nature of Christ can be in more than one place at the same time. The Roman Catholic view essentially attributes the quality of omni-

presence to the physical body of Jesus. If the Mass is being celebrated simultaneously in New York, Chicago, and Los Angeles,
then, according to Roman Catholic teaching, His physical body and
blood, which are part of His human nature, not part of His divine
nature, are present in more than one place at the same time. Rome
says this happens because there is a communication of power from
the divine nature, which can be omnipresent, to the human nature.
But once the human nature assumes the attributes of the divine
nature, Rome has a problem with her own Christology. The Council of Chalcedon (451) defined the relationship of the two natures
of Christ, saying that He is *vera homo vera deus*, that is, "truly man
and truly God," and that the two natures are in perfect unity but
without mixture, confusion, separation, or division, so that each
nature retains its own attributes. So, Rome needs to explain how
attributing omnipresence to the body of Christ does not involve a
deification of the flesh of Jesus, giving it a divine attribute. How
does that not confuse the two natures of Christ?

In modern times, there has been some reaction within the
Roman Church against the concept of transubstantiation, particularly sparked by the Flemish theologian Edward Schillebeeckx
(1914–2009). He wrote a book called *Christ, the Sacrament of the
Encounter with God*, in which he argued that the church should set
aside the old formulas of Aristotle. He sought to restate the doctrine
in modern terms, abandoning the term *transubstantiation* in favor of
transignification. According to his view, the actual body and blood of
Jesus are not physically present in the bread and wine, but they are
really and objectively there. Thus, at the consecration, the bread and
wine take on the real significance of the body and blood.

However, in 1965, Pope Paul VI released an encyclical on the
Eucharist, *Mysterium Fidei* ("The Mystery of the Faith"), that dis-
missed Schillebeeckx's ideas and strongly reaffirmed the traditional
Roman Catholic understanding of the Lord's Supper. He said:

The Church, therefore, with the long labor of centuries and, not without the help of the Holy Spirit, has established a rule of language and confirmed it with the authority of the councils. This rule, which has more than once been the watchword and banner of Orthodox faith, must be religiously preserved, and let no one presume to change it at his own pleasure or under the pretext of new science. Who would ever tolerate that the dogmatic formulas used by the ecumenical councils for the mysteries of the Holy Trinity and the Incarnation be judged as no longer appropriate for men of our times and therefore that others be rashly substituted for them? In the same way it cannot be tolerated that any individual should on his own authority modify the formulas which were used by the Council of Trent to express belief in the Eucharistic Mystery.[2]

Roman Catholic and Protestant affirmations

In like manner, Rome reaffirmed many of its traditional stances on the sacraments in the recent edition of the Catechism of the Catholic Church (1995). Here are the catechism's words in regard to some of the more controversial topics we have discussed:

The Church affirms that for believers the sacraments of the New Covenant are necessary for salvation. (Section 1129)

Christ instituted the sacraments of the new law. There are seven: Baptism, Confirmation (or Chrismation), the Eucharist, Penance, the Anointing of the Sick, Holy Orders and Matrimony. The seven sacraments touch all the stages and all the important moments of Christian life: they give birth and increase, healing and mission to the Christian's life of faith. There is thus a certain resemblance between the stages of natural life and the stages of the spiritual life. (1210)

Holy Baptism is the basis of the whole Christian life, the gateway to life in the Spirit (*vitae spiritualis ianua*), and the door which gives access to the other sacraments. Through Baptism we are freed from sin and reborn as sons of God; we become members of Christ, are incorporated into the Church and made sharers in her mission. (1213)

By Baptism all sins are forgiven, original sin and all personal sins, as well as all punishment for sin. In those who have been reborn nothing remains that would impede their entry into the Kingdom of God, neither Adam's sin, nor personal sin, nor the consequences of sin, the gravest of which is separation from God. (1263)

Baptism, the Eucharist, and the sacrament of Confirmation together constitute the "sacraments of Christian initiation," whose unity must be safeguarded. It must be explained to the faithful that the reception of the sacrament of Confirmation is necessary for the completion of baptismal grace. For "by the sacrament of Confirmation, [the baptized] are more perfectly bound to the Church and are enriched with a special strength of the Holy Spirit." (1285)

At the heart of the Eucharistic celebration are the bread and wine that, by the words of Christ and the invocation of the Holy Spirit, become Christ's Body and Blood. (1333)

Many sins wrong our neighbor. One must do what is possible in order to repair the harm (e.g., return stolen goods, restore the reputation of someone slandered, pay compensation for injuries). Simple justice requires as much. But sin also injures and weakens the sinner himself, as well as his relationships with God and neighbor. Absolution takes away sin, but it does not remedy all the disorders sin has caused. Raised up from sin, the sinner must still recover his full spiritual health by doing something more to make amends for the sin; he must make "satisfaction for" or "expiate" his sins. This satisfaction is also called "penance." (1459)

An indulgence is obtained through the Church who, by virtue of the power of binding and loosing granted her by Christ Jesus, intervenes in favor of individual Christians and opens for them the treasury of the merits of Christ and the saints to obtain from the Father of mercies the remission of the temporal punishments due for their sins. (1478)

Over against these statements, here are the positions the Reformers took on some of these issues, as stated in the Westminster Confession of Faith:

There be only two sacraments ordained by Christ our Lord in the gospels, that is to say, Baptism and the Supper of the Lord: neither of which may be dispensed by any but a minister of the Word, lawfully ordained. (27.4)

Although it be a great sin to contemn or neglect [baptism], yet grace and salvation are not so inseparably annexed unto it as that no person can be regenerated or saved without it, or that all that are baptized are undoubtedly regenerated. (28.5)

In [the Lord's Supper] Christ is not offered up to his Father, nor any real sacrifice made at all for remission of sins of the quick or dead, but a commemoration of that one offering up of himself, by himself, upon the cross, once for all, and a spiritual oblation of all possible praise unto God for the same; so that the Popish sacrifice of the mass, as they call it, is most abominably injurious to Christ's one and only sacrifice, the only propitiation for all the sins of the elect. (29.2)

Private masses, or receiving this sacrament by a priest, or any other, alone; as likewise the denial of the cup to the people; worshipping the elements, the lifting them up, or carrying them about for adoration, and the reserving them for any pretended religious use, are all contrary to the nature of this sacrament, and to the institution of Christ. (29.4)

The outward elements in this sacrament, duly set apart to the uses ordained by Christ, have such relation to him crucified, as that truly, yet sacramentally only, they are sometimes called by the name of the things they represent, to wit, the body and blood of Christ; albeit, in substance and nature, they still remain truly, and only, bread and wine, as they were before. (29.5)

That doctrine which maintains a change of the substance of bread and wine, into the substance of Christ's body and blood (commonly called transubstantiation) by consecration of a priest, or by any other way, is repugnant, not to Scripture alone, but even to common-sense and reason; overthroweth the nature of the sacrament; and hath been, and is, the cause of manifold superstitions, yea, of gross idolatries. (29.6)

I believe these quotations make it manifestly clear that nothing has changed, either on the Protestant side or the Roman Catholic side, to erase the longstanding differences over the sacraments. Rome's view remains riddled with errors and superstitions.

Particularly in its continuing insistence that baptism conveys the grace of justification and its teaching that the body of Christ is broken anew each time the Mass is celebrated, Rome is proclaiming things that are repugnant to those who believe and trust the Word of God.

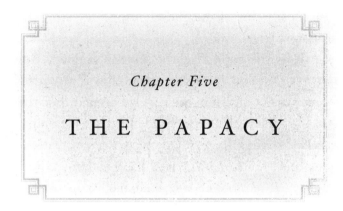

Chapter Five

THE PAPACY

ON JULY 18, 1870, AS PART of the ecumenical council known as Vatican I, the Roman Catholic Church formally defined the doctrine of papal infallibility. It was declared to be *de fide* ("of the faith"), that is, an official doctrine of the church, the denial of which would constitute heresy. The vote in the council to elevate this doctrine to *de fide* status was 533 to 2.

So, the formal proclamation of the doctrine of papal infallibility is a relatively recent development, one that came long after the Protestant Reformation. However, the concept of papal infallibility and the conviction as to the truth of it have roots very early in church history. So, it will be helpful to briefly review the historical background leading up to the developments at Vatican I.

As we see in the book of Acts, the church began in Jerusalem, and Jerusalem was its focal point in its early years. It was there that the first church council was held to settle the question of the Judaizers (Acts 15). However, Acts ends with the Apostle Paul going to Rome. No one knows who founded the church in Rome, but it soon became the focal point of the church, especially after the destruction of Jerusalem in AD 70.

Obviously, as the capital of the Roman Empire, Rome was a very important city, and the Roman church was accorded a unique status because of its location. Some have argued that the church's presence in the capital also influenced how its leadership structures developed. Hans Küng (b. 1928), a Swiss Roman Catholic theologian, argues that the primary reason the Roman Catholic Church developed in the direction of a monarchial episcopate and papal primacy was because it was carried along on the coattails of the Roman governmental system. He believes the church simply adopted many of the political and juridical structures of the Roman government, which the church members observed every day of their lives.

It is not difficult to find indications of the importance of the church in Rome. Paul's epistle to the Romans is of great weight and significance, and we know Paul was eager to minister there (Rom. 1:11, 13; 15:23) and expected the Roman church to help him on a journey to Spain (15:24, 28). Tradition has it—and there is much extrabiblical evidence to support it—that both Paul and the Apostle Peter were martyred in Rome around AD 65 during Emperor Nero's persecutions. All things considered, it is not surprising that the leader of this congregation in the capital of the empire came to be regarded as an important leader in the entire Christian movement in the very early years of the church.

One of the sources that shows us the early prominence of the leaders of the Roman church is the first epistle of Clement. This extrabiblical letter, usually dated around the year 95, was written by one who is identified as the bishop of Rome. According to tradition, Clement was the fourth such bishop, following Peter, Linus, and Anacletus. Clement wrote his epistle to the church at Corinth, to which Paul wrote at least two letters, the New Testament books of 1 and 2 Corinthians. First Corinthians is filled with admonitions to a very troubled church. Second Corinthians shows that the Corinthian church heeded many of Paul's admonitions in his first letter, but troubles remained, including false prophets who were challenging Paul's authority. Sometimes we wonder how the Corinthian church fared in the long term. Did it deal effectively with the sin and divisions in its ranks in response to Paul's admonitions, or did it continue to experience troubles?

Sadly, 1 Clement indicates that the church did not fare well, because it became necessary about forty years later for the bishop of Rome to intervene in a situation in the Corinthian congregation. It seems there was a problem of ecclesiastical organization and that there had been a revolt by some who believed they had been gifted by the Spirit and directed by God to overthrow the regular officers of the church. So, Clement, the bishop of Rome, wrote a letter beseeching the people who had been carried away in their religious zeal to get their act together.

One church historian, in analyzing 1 Clement, says that the letter is written in a spirit of brotherly love and admonition rather than an autocratic, tyrannical tone. But, the historian says, though it is written in a brotherly motif, it is a big-brotherly motif. I think that is an excellent description of the tone of 1 Clement. Clement does not sound like a twentieth-century pope delivering an encyclical that commands the Corinthian people to repent on the strength of his office. Rather, he justifies his pastoral concern for the situation in Corinth as the concern of a shepherd, one who has the right to exercise spiritual oversight of and give a pastoral admonition to a congregation outside his geographical jurisdiction.

Over the centuries, there was a gradual increase of the power and authority of the bishop of Rome. For example, in the controversies of the fourth century, the theological debates between Pelagius and Augustine in North Africa, the local church authorities appealed at one point for a decision by the bishop of Rome. As time passed, the popes began to assert a claim of universal jurisdiction over all the churches. This claim was especially resented in the eastern areas of the empire. Finally, in 1054, a group of papal representatives traveled to Constantinople to insist that Michael Cerularius, the patriarch of Constantinople, recognize the church in Rome as the mother church. He refused, sparking the Great Schism, the division of the Roman Catholic and Eastern Orthodox churches, a breach that has never been healed.

Gallicanism and ultramontanism

By the nineteenth century, two significant philosophical trends came to the fore that would have a significant impact at Vatican Council I. First, there was the phenomenon of Gallicanism. This school of thought originated in thirteenth-century France, which explains the origin of the term *Gallicanism*: "Gaul" was the name of the region that, during Roman times, encompassed modern-day France and some surrounding regions. Gallicanism began with the resistance of French Christians to Roman rule. The church of France wanted to govern its own affairs rather than take orders from the pope. That effort failed, but Gallicanism continued and became the moniker for all such efforts at self-government. When it reached its peak in the nineteenth century, Gallicanism was the term for any aspiration for home rule without papal intervention. This was not merely an ecclesiastical power struggle, but an ecclesiastical-political power struggle, because in many of the nations of Europe at that time there was no separation of church and state. And, of course, the papacy still had considerable political power at that time.

Second, there was the school of thought known as ultramontanism. The word *ultramontanism* literally means "across the mountains." This term was applied to those who opposed Gallicanism and were in favor of authority centered in Rome, which was across the Alps from France. Ultramontanism favored a centralized ecclesiastical government for the Roman Catholic Church, with the pope holding supreme episcopal power.

In June 1846, Giovanni Maria Mastai-Ferretti was elected as Pope Pius IX, beginning the longest papacy ever, thirty-two years. When Pius came to power, he was regarded as somewhat liberal, certainly not as an ultramontanist. But during the early years of his papacy, several of the programs of reform that he tried to institute failed, and he went through something of a personal crisis. As a result, he became a total reactionary and a staunch opponent of the Gallicanist movement, and he began to press very hard for consolidation of the strength of the papacy.

In 1854, Pius unilaterally, without consulting the College of Cardinals or the bishops, issued *Ineffabilis Deus* ("Ineffable God"), a papal encyclical in which he declared the immaculate conception of Mary (the teaching that Mary had no original sin) and declared it a *de fide* doctrine. I will spend more time examining this encyclical and the whole subject of Mariology in chapter 6, but I simply mention it here to show Pius' growing tendency to rule the church in an autocratic manner. He took a similar action in 1864 when he published the "Syllabus of Errors," which condemned a long list of propositions, including naturalism, evolutionism, liberalism, and separation of church and state. This document was also a scathing denunciation of Protestantism. It specifically denied the proposition that "Protestantism is nothing more than another form of the same true Christian religion, in which form it is given to please God equally as in the Catholic Church."[1] Naturally, Pius and the church came under intense Protestant criticism for this stance.

In the decade before Vatican I, significant political events occurred that were to have a momentous effect on the council's decrees. In 1860, Victor Emanuel II, king of Italy, defeated the pope's military forces and captured most papal lands, leaving Pius in control of little more than the Vatican. Pius promptly excommunicated Victor Emanuel, but the king refused to bow to the pope's wishes. However, these setbacks had the effect of creating enormous popular sympathy for Pius. Financial campaigns were launched to help the papacy, and in the end Pius' finances were in better shape than before he lost the papal states. He also continued to enjoy significant popular support and veneration from Roman Catholic peoples worldwide.

Küng, the Swiss theologian, who has been somewhat critical of the papacy, had this to say in regard to Pius' popularity:

Although Pius IX . . . brought the Italian Catholics into unnecessary severe conflicts of conscience, he won tremendous sympathy for his person and his office in the role of a man persecuted by unchristian powers. The dogmatic bond of Catholics to the pope now acquired a sentimental touch. A completely new phenomenon arose: a highly emotional "veneration of the pope," which was considerably strengthened by the now customary papal audiences and mass pilgrimages to Rome. Pius IX, a philanthropic, very eloquent, strongly radiant personality, but dangerously emotional, superficially trained in theology, and completely unfamiliar with modern scientific methods, badly advised moreover by zealous but mediocre, unrealistic and dogmatically minded associates, saw the crisis of the papal states simply as an episode in the universal history of the struggle between God and Satan, and hoped to overcome it with an almost mystical confidence in the victory of divine providence.[2]

So, when Pius convened Vatican I in 1869, the papacy was under siege by secular authorities but enjoying popular support.

Decisions of Vatican I

The primacy of the pope was established in the Fourth Session of Vatican I, the decisions of which are stated in "The First Dogmatic Constitution on the Church of Christ" (July 18, 1870). It is worth our time to consider some of the statements from this document. The introduction stated:

> And since the gates of hell trying, if they can, to overthrow the church, make their assault with a hatred that increases day by day against its divinely laid foundation, we judge it necessary, with the approbation of the sacred council, and for the protection, defence and growth of the catholic flock, to propound the doctrine concerning the 1. institution, 2. permanence and 3. nature of the sacred and apostolic primacy, upon which the strength and coherence of the whole church depends. This doctrine is to be believed and held by all the faithful in accordance with the ancient and unchanging faith of the whole church. Furthermore, we shall proscribe and condemn the contrary errors which are so harmful to the Lord's flock.[3]

Notice the insistence that "this doctrine is to be believed and held by all the faithful." Sometimes papal encyclicals and conciliar statements say that a particular doctrine is to be held by all faithful Roman Catholics. But here the doctrine of papal infallibility was required not only to be held but to be believed.

Most conciliar statements not only make declarations, they also proscribe errors. For instance, the Council of Trent said, "If any one saith, that by faith alone the impious is justified; in such wise as to mean, that nothing else is required to co-operate in order to the obtaining the grace of Justification, and that it is not in any way necessary, that he be prepared and disposed by the movement of his own will; let him be anathema."[4] The word *anathema*, of course, means "cursed" or "excommunicated."

The statements of Vatican I also included anathemas. In the first chapter of the Dogmatic Constitution, the council defined the primacy of Peter, declaring that he was not simply one of the Apostles, but that Jesus gave him primacy over all the other Apostles of the early church. At the end of that chapter, the council declared: "Therefore, if anyone says that blessed Peter the apostle was not appointed by Christ the lord as prince of all the apostles and visible head of the whole church militant; or that it was a primacy of honour only and not one of true and proper jurisdiction that he directly and immediately received from our lord Jesus Christ himself: let him be anathema."[5]

Likewise, the council asserted that Peter's primacy has been passed on in a perpetual succession, and this belief is essential: "If anyone says that it is not by the institution of Christ the lord himself (that is to say, by divine law) that blessed Peter should have perpetual successors in the primacy over the whole church; or that the Roman pontiff is not the successor of blessed Peter in this primacy: let him be anathema."[6] So, not only is there a succession of bishops, but Peter's primacy is passed along as well.

Finally, the council said:

If anyone says that the Roman pontiff has merely an office of supervision and guidance, and not the full and supreme power of jurisdiction over the whole church, and this not only in matters of faith and morals, but also in those which concern the discipline and the government of the church dispersed throughout the whole world; or that he has only the principal part, but not the absolute fullness, of this supreme power; or that this power of his is not ordinary and immediate both over all and each of the churches and over all and each of the pastors and faithful: let him be anathema.[7]

That is, papal authority is not merely teaching authority, it is a governmental authority. Thus, the pope has jurisdiction over the discipline and government of the whole church. This is what Roman Catholics call the primacy of jurisdiction.

The definition of infallibility

It is in the fourth and last chapter of the Dogmatic Constitution that we find the definition of papal infallibility. It states:

> We teach and define as a divinely revealed dogma that when the Roman pontiff speaks EX CATHEDRA, that is, when, in the exercise of his office as shepherd and teacher of all Christians, in virtue of his supreme apostolic authority, he defines a doctrine concerning faith or morals to be held by the whole church, he possesses, by the divine assistance promised to him in blessed Peter, that infallibility which the divine Redeemer willed his church to enjoy in defining doctrine concerning faith or morals. Therefore, such definitions of the Roman pontiff are of themselves, and not by the consent of the church, irreformable.[8]

There are two key concepts in this definition. First, papal infallibility is restricted to those utterances of the pope on faith or morals that are given *ex cathedra*, that is, when he is giving a decision on behalf of the whole church. Therefore, Vatican I was not saying that if we encountered the pope on the streets of Rome and asked him for directions to the nearest pizza parlor, we could assume that he would give impeccably accurate directions. He might send us to the wrong street or even to the wrong section of the city. The pope is eminently fallible with respect to such everyday matters. In other words, the council did not proclaim an infallibility of person, merely an infallibility of office only when the pope speaks on matters of faith and morals, speaking from his official chair, exercising the office of the pope. Second, according to this statement, papal infallibility is not intrinsic; rather, it comes through the divine assistance promised to the pope in Peter. He can be infallible when speaking on faith or morals because of special divine assistance given to him.

Great controversy has followed the last line: "Therefore, such definitions of the Roman pontiff are of themselves, and not by the consent of the church, irreformable." The question here is whether the pope speaks *ex sese*—that is, "out of himself"—or whether he speaks out of the broader context of the whole church. Is papal infallibility something that the pope can exercise unilaterally or must it be done in consultation with and in a spirit of collegiality with the bishops and cardinals of the church? Vatican I never answered this question because the council ended prematurely due to the invasion of Rome by Victor Emanuel II. So, the participants were not able to tie up all the loose ends.

Reactions to the pronouncements of Vatican I varied sharply. On one hand, there were those who strongly applauded the doctrine of the infallibility of the pope. These individuals began to hail this new teaching with extravagant statements that implied that the pope *did* have intrinsic infallibility. Some even made comparisons of the infallibility of God and the infallibility of the pope. On the other hand, many were strongly opposed to this doctrine. The leading German theologian and historian of the day, Johan Josef Ignaz von Döllinger, refused to accept this decree of infallibility, for which he was summarily excommunicated. Also, a group of Roman Catholics withdrew from the communion and formed what has come to be known as the Old Catholic Church. By 1950, there were more than a hundred thousand adherents in this group. The Old Catholic

Church, which is found substantially in Germany, Switzerland, Holland, and Austria, is Roman Catholic in virtually every respect except it does not recognize the primacy of the pope.

In 1872, Otto von Bismarck, chancellor of the new German Empire, came under criticism from some of the local bishops over his policies. He declared that he did not need to pay attention to the bishops because they were only "hirelings" who lacked power and authority. Bismarck had interpreted Vatican I as essentially leaving the bishops with no power. In his eyes, they were insignificant compared with the pope. The bishops responded very indignantly, saying that they had received their authority directly and immediately from Jesus Christ, in whose name and authority they spoke. Essentially, the controversy was over the final clause of Vatican I's Dogmatic Constitution. That same year, Pius IX affirmed that the bishops did indeed have their authority directly and immediately from Christ and that they were not excluded from the authority of the church by the doctrine of papal infallibility. But the precise balance of power was not defined.

Clarifications at Vatican II

Not surprisingly, this question came up again at Vatican II. In the section of Vatican II titled *Lumen Gentium* ("Light of the Nations"), the Dogmatic Constitution on the Church, the infallibility of the pope was treated in some detail. As noted earlier, the basic spirit of Vatican II was radically different from Vatican I. Vatican I took place in the context of fear and emotional upheaval. Vatican II took place amid a spirit of conciliation and irenicism. For example, Vatican I referred to Protestants as schismatic and heretics. By contrast, Vatican II spoke of Protestants as separated brethren. Pope John XXIII declared it was time to open the windows of the church so fresh air could blow in, by which he meant that a fresh spirit of humility should characterize this council.

Despite this conciliation and warmth, however, *Lumen Gentium* offered a strong confirmation of Vatican I regarding the primacy and infallibility of the pope. It added nuances that resolved some of the questions about the respective power and authority of the pope and the bishops, but it did not at all diminish Vatican I's affirmation of the infallibility of the pope with regard to matters of faith and morals. It is worth taking a brief overview of the major statements of *Lumen Gentium*.

First, the council said, "This Sacred Council, following closely in the footsteps of the First Vatican Council, with that Council teaches and declares that Jesus Christ, the eternal Shepherd, established His holy Church, having sent forth the apostles as He Himself had been sent by the Father; and He willed that their successors, namely the bishops, should be shepherds in His Church even to the consummation of the world."[9] All of the bishops of the church were said to be successors of the Apostles. The pope is the successor of Peter, the first of the Apostles, and the bishops are the successors of the other Apostles. Thus, the bishops are not "hirelings," as Bismarck declared; rather, they are as significant as the other Apostles who served under Peter.

Second, the council proclaimed that the authority of the bishop is by ordination and consecration, not by papal confirmation or appointment: "For the discharging of such great duties, the apostles were enriched by Christ with a special outpouring of the Holy Spirit coming upon them, and they passed on this spiritual gift to their helpers by the imposition of hands, and it has been transmitted down to us in Episcopal consecration. And the Sacred Council teaches that by Episcopal consecration the fullness of the sacrament of Orders is conferred, that fullness of power, namely, which both in the Church's liturgical practice and in the language of the Fathers of the church is called the high priesthood, the supreme power of the sacred ministry."[10] Why did the council take such pains to teach that the authority of the office of bishop resides in the sacrament of his holy orders? It was to show that the bishops' power and authority came from God through the sacraments, not from papal authority.

Third, the council said, "Although the individual bishops do not enjoy the prerogative of infallibility, they nevertheless proclaim Christ's doctrine infallibly whenever, even though dispersed through the world, but still maintaining the bond of communion among themselves and with the successor of Peter, and authentically teaching matters of faith and morals, they are in agreement on one position as definitively to be held."[11] So, while the pope has the prerogative of infallibility, individual bishops do not. However, the bishops can proclaim Christian doctrine infallibly—if they are united with the pope, concur on a single viewpoint, or agree in an ecumenical council with the pope. Under those circumstances, they more or less participate in infallibility with the pope. It is a collegial concept, a corporate concept, not an individual concept of infallibility. That is reserved for the pope.

This teaching has several implications. First, there are limits on papal infallibility. There is primacy but not absolutism. There are certain things that, by canon law, the pope may not do. For example, he cannot unilaterally abolish the episcopacy or usurp the office and ministry of the bishops. He cannot write an encyclical and claim that he has infallibly decided to put an end to the bishops and depose them. If a pope tried to do that, the church could depose him, because since Vatican II the notion is that the pope's infallibility is a localized trait that extends to the whole church. It focuses on him, but it does not reside in him intrinsically.

Second, the power of the pope is not arbitrary. The papacy is to be understood as a ministry, not a dominion. Vatican I referred to the pope as the head of the body of Christ or the head of the church. But if Christ is the Head of the church, how can the pope be the head of the church—is not the pope usurping the position that is given to Christ alone? This is why Vatican II spoke of the pope as the shepherd of the flock or the vicar of Christ, or Christ's head on earth. In that sense, he is the head of the church, being the representative or substitute of the leadership of Jesus; but Christ, of course, is the true Head of the church.

Third, the pope shares with the bishops collegial responsibility for the governing of the church. His governance is not to be done unilaterally without consultation with the bishops.

Roman Catholic and Protestant affirmations

The Roman Catholic Church continues to affirm these teachings. The Catechism of the Catholic Church (1995) declares:

> "The Roman Pontiff, head of the college of bishops, enjoys . . . infallibility in virtue of his office, when, as supreme pastor and teacher of all the faithful—who confirms his brethren in the faith—he proclaims by a definitive act a doctrine pertaining to faith or morals. . . . The infallibility promised to the church is also present in the body of bishops when, together with Peter's successor, they exercise the supreme Magisterium," above all in an Ecumenical Council. When the Church through its supreme Magisterium proposes a doctrine "for belief as being divinely revealed," and as the teaching of Christ, the definitions "must be adhered to with the obedience of faith." This infallibility extends as far as the deposit of divine Revelation itself. (Section 891)

The great Reformation confessions and creeds were written before the doctrine of papal infallibility was formulated, but it is important to remember what the Reformers believed about the papacy. The Westminster Confession of Faith says:

The catholic or universal church, which is invisible, consists of the whole number of the elect, that have been, are, or shall be gathered into one, under Christ the Head thereof; and is the spouse, the body, the fullness of him that filleth all in all. (25:1)

There is no other head of the church but the Lord Jesus Christ. Nor can the pope of Rome, in any sense, be head thereof. (25:6)

We do well to remember that only one Man has ever spoken infallibly—our Lord Jesus, who alone is Head of His church. Let us receive His Word—the Scriptures—as the only infallible communication from God.

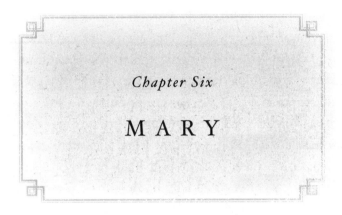

Chapter Six

MARY

THE ROMAN CATHOLIC VIEW OF Mary, the mother of Jesus, has been the subject of much controversy and debate, not only between Protestants and Roman Catholics, but also within the Roman Catholic Church. Like the notion of papal infallibility, many Roman Catholic teachings on Mariology were not formally defined until well after the Reformation. In fact, in the case of Mary, most of the definitions were laid down in 1854 and again in 1950. However, preoccupation with the person and work of Mary is of great age and lengthy tradition within the Roman Catholic Church.

Popular manifestations of the Mary cultus within the Roman Catholic Church are not difficult to find. Perhaps the most obvious manifestation of the church's veneration of Mary can be seen in art. Medieval art and to some degree Renaissance art are dominated by portrayals of the Madonna, and quite often the Madonna and Child or the Madonna assisting in the descent of Christ from the cross. At the Vatican, there is an outstanding fresco that features the Madonna high and exalted, with Christ and the Father seated on either side of her. Likewise, we see the celebration of Mary in the music of the church historically. Several hymns are devoted to her, the most famous of which is the *"Ave Maria,"* or the "Hail Mary."

A number of shrines are dedicated to the veneration of Mary throughout the world. There are two kinds of shrines. First, there are private shrines. These were quite popular in earlier decades; at one time, a Roman Catholic household was not considered to be doing its full duty unless it had some kind of garden shrine, a statue in the yard, or a private place for the celebration of Mary. Second, there are public shrines to which people may make sanctioned pilgrimages, by which a person who is working through the penance process may earn satisfaction.

Among the public shrines, the most famous include Fatima, Portugal, where Mary is said to have appeared to three shepherd children in 1917. In the summer of that year, a huge crowd reportedly witnessed the so-called "miracle of the sun," in which the sun seemed to dance in the sky and display multiple colors. Many people who have visited the shrine of Our Lady of Fatima have said they received miraculous cures.

Another famous public shrine is in Lourdes, France, where a teenage girl, Bernadette Soubirous, reported that a beautiful woman appeared to her a number of times in 1858. Roman Catholics believe this woman was Mary, although she never identified herself as such. However, in one of these appearances, the woman called herself "the immaculate conception." It is interesting that Pope Pius IX had promulgated the doctrine of the immaculate conception—about which I will say more below—in 1854, four years before Bernadette's visions at Lourdes.

Much more could be said about the popular view of Mary. Celebrations in her honor are held regularly within the church, including the Feast of the immaculate conception on December 8. Countless schools and churches have been named in her honor, as have orders of mission helpers, nuns, and so forth. She is, to say the least, a major figure in the faith of ordinary Roman Catholics.

"Hail Mary, full of grace"

One of the aspects of Roman Catholic veneration of Mary is the series of prayers that make up the Rosary. The "Hail Mary" is at the heart of the Rosary. Its traditional wording is as follows: "Hail Mary, full of grace, the Lord is with thee; blessed art thou among women, and blessed is the fruit of thy womb, Jesus. Holy Mary, mother of God, pray for us sinners, now and at the hour of our death. Amen." As we begin to analyze the Roman Catholic view of Mary, I want to look closely at these words. In doing so, we will begin to see the outlines of the controversy between Protestantism and Roman Catholicism.

The words, "Hail Mary, full of grace, the Lord is with thee; blessed art thou among women, and blessed is the fruit of thy womb, Jesus," come from Scripture. This sentence incorporates the words of the angel who announced God's plans to Mary (Luke 1:28) and the words of Elizabeth, when she greeted Mary (v. 42). Thus, these words themselves could never be repugnant to a Protestant who holds to the authority of Scripture. However, the use of the words in the form of a prayer does raise questions for us.

The second sentence of the "Hail Mary" is much more problematic: "Holy Mary, mother of God, pray for us sinners, now and at the hour of our death. Amen." Protestants do not object to calling Mary "holy." After all, we refer to believers as "saints" in the sense of being set apart. All Christians are "holy" in that sense. Thus, saying Mary is "holy" does not necessarily indicate we are worshiping her.

What about the phrase "mother of God"? The Council of Ephesus (431) gave Mary the Greek title *Theotokos*, which literally means "God-bearer" or "the one who gives birth to God." Taken less literally, it is usually rendered "mother of God." This title was ratified at the Council of Chalcedon (451), the one ecumenical council that is endorsed by virtually every church in the World Council of Churches. But what does this title really mean?

At the time of the Council of Ephesus, *Theotokos* was understood to mean that Mary was the mother of God, but not in the sense that Jesus received His divine nature from Mary in any way. It simply meant that Mary, being the mother of Jesus, was the mother of God in that sense—Jesus is God and Mary is His mother, touching His human nature. There was no confusion at Ephesus or Chalcedon that this title was meant to ascribe any notion of deity to Mary. It simply articulated the fact that she was the earthly mother of the One who was God incarnate. Historian Jaroslav Pelikan has given a very good translation of *Theotokos*, one that accurately captures this historical understanding: "the one who gives birth to the One who is God."[1] Given this understanding, historically there has been no official Protestant objection to the title "mother of God." Obviously, this title could be understood to mean much more than it was understood to mean at Ephesus and at Chalcedon, but the words in and of themselves, properly qualified and defined, are not an occasion of controversy.

The "Hail Mary" concludes with a petition for Mary to "pray for us sinners, now and at the hour of our death." Here we have a problem. Attributing intercessory work to Mary draws objections from the vast majority of Protestants. They argue that viewing Mary as one who intercedes for us either now or at our deaths makes Mary a kind of mediator of our redemption. Generally speaking, Protestantism insists that Jesus is the sole Mediator between God and man (1 Tim. 2:5), although, of course, the Holy Spirit also intercedes for us (Rom. 8:26).

Pronouncements about Mary

With that background, I want to look now at the church's official pronouncements concerning Mary. As I noted earlier, many of the official teachings on Mary are very recent, but they did not happen suddenly; there was a long history of development of veneration of Mary within the Roman Catholic Church.

Let me begin with the doctrine of the immaculate conception, which was mentioned just above. This doctrine was officially declared in a papal encyclical in 1854. Many Protestants believe that "immaculate conception" refers to the virgin birth of Jesus. However, the doctrine of the virgin birth has been a tenet of all Christendom since the early days of the church, one that Protestants joyfully embrace along with Roman Catholics, so there would have been no need for Pius IX to officially affirm it in 1854. The doctrine of the immaculate conception actually has to do with Mary's own conception. It is the belief that Mary was not infected with original sin at her conception, so she lived a sinless life.

This doctrine, of course, has drawn strong objections from Protestants. One problem is that if Mary was sinless, she did not need a Redeemer. Also, if she had no sin, she was herself fit to be the champion of our redemption in some degree. Indeed, this doctrine has fueled the view in Roman Catholic circles that Mary is our Co-Redemptrix, that she participated in the redemptive process. This title has not been officially sanctioned by the Roman Catholic Church, and it is much disputed in Rome, but many hold this view of Mary.

The supreme theologian of the Roman Catholic Church, the Doctor Angelicus, Thomas Aquinas (1225–74) repudiated the notion of the sinlessness of Mary in his day. The fact that Thomas wrote about this idea shows that there was a public movement as early as the Middle Ages to regard Mary as sinless. Thomas took his stand against this teaching on the basis of Mary's words in the *Magnificat*: "My soul magnifies the Lord, and my spirit has rejoiced in God my Savior" (Luke 1:46–47). Thomas said that in this song of thanksgiving and praise, which was inspired by the Holy Spirit, Mary confessed her need for a Savior, indicating that she was sinful. So, the Roman

Catholic Church was faced with the embarrassing situation that its supreme theologian denied this doctrine.

How did the church respond? First, Rome noted that Thomas was speaking before the doctrine was defined. He was a great theologian, to be sure, but he was not infallible, and if he had seen how the church defined the doctrine of the immaculate conception, he certainly would have believed it on the basis of a *fide implicitum*, that is, an implicit faith in whatever the church declares. Second, it was suggested that he may have been wrong. The exegetes of Rome pointed out that the term *Savior* does not always mean one who saves from sin. A person can be saved from other things, and salvation can be understood in a much broader sense, as an experience of benefits at the hands of God. Indeed, Mary did receive great benefits, and in that sense God was her Savior; that is, He was her Benefactor. He gave certain blessings to her that He gave to no one else. This is a possible interpretation of that passage from the *Magnificat*, although I think it is somewhat forced linguistically.

In 1950, in a document called an Apostolic constitution, *Munificentissimus Deus* ("The Most Bountiful God"), Pope Pius XII defined the doctrine of the bodily assumption of Mary into heaven, the idea that Mary was taken up into heaven bodily and that she already participates fully in the resurrection of the body, to which all believers look forward. Likewise, in 1954, Pius issued an encyclical, *Ad Caeli Reginam* ("Queen of Heaven"), that instituted the feast Queenship of Mary, establishing as the official teaching of the church that Mary reigns as queen of heaven alongside her Son, King Jesus.

A call to veneration of Mary

The call to give veneration to Mary has come from the highest levels of the church. Perhaps the most direct papal treatment of this idea is found in Pius XII's 1943 encyclical *Mystici Corporis Christi* ("The Mystical Body of Christ"). Near the end, Pius stated:

Venerable Brethren, may the Virgin Mother of God hear the prayers of Our paternal heart—which are yours also—and obtain for all a true love of the Church—she whose sinless soul was filled with the divine Spirit of Jesus Christ above all other created souls, and who "in the name of the whole human race" gave her consent "for a spiritual marriage between the Son of God and human nature." Within her virginal womb Christ our Lord already bore the exalted title of Head of the Church; in a marvelous birth she brought Him forth as the source of all supernatural life, and presented Him, newly born, as Prophet, King, and Priest to those who, from among Jews and Gentiles, were the first to come to adore Him. Furthermore, her only Son, condescending to His mother's prayer in "Cana of Galilee," performed the miracle by which "his disciples believed in him." It was she, the second Eve, who, free from all sin, original or personal, and always most intimately united with her Son, offered Him on Golgotha to the Eternal Father for all the children of Adam, sin-stained by his unhappy fall, and her mother's rights and mother's love were included in the holocaust."[2]

What did Pius mean when he affirmed that Mary "offered Him on Golgotha to the Eternal Father"? Was he thinking merely of the sacrificial presentation of a mother of her son? Or was he thinking of a priestly offering? If it was simply the offering of a mother of the son, I can only say that the pope was extremely ill-advised to use the word *offered*, which is loaded with theological connotations.

Pius continued: "Thus she who, according to the flesh, was the mother of our Head, through the added title of pain and glory became, according to the Spirit, the mother of all His members."[3] This statement makes Mary the mother of the church as well as the mother of Christ.

He added: "She it was who through her powerful prayers obtained that the Spirit of our Divine Redeemer, already given on the Cross, should be bestowed, accompanied by miraculous gifts, on the newly founded Church at Pentecost."[4] Who was mediatorially responsible for the outpouring of the Holy Spirit at Pentecost? According to Pius, the powerful prayers of Mary obtained this blessing for the church.

Continuing, he wrote: "Finally bearing with courage and confidence the tremendous burden of her sorrows and desolation, she, truly the Queen of Martyrs, more than all the faithful 'filled up those things that are wanting of the sufferings of Christ . . . for His Body, which is the Church'; and she continues to have for the Mystical Body of Christ, born of the pierced Heart of the Saviour, the same motherly care and ardent love with which she cherished and fed the Infant Jesus in the crib."[5] Mary still cares for the church of Jesus Christ in an analogous way to the care she gave Jesus when she fed and nourished Him as an infant.

Pius concluded:

May she, then, the most holy Mother of all the members of Christ, to whose Immaculate Heart We have trustfully consecrated all mankind, and who now reigns in heaven with her Son, her body and soul refulgent with heavenly glory—may she never cease to beg from Him that copious streams of grace may flow from its exalted Head into all the members of the Mystical Body. May she throw about the Church today, as in times gone by, the mantle of her protection and obtain from God that now at last the Church and all mankind may enjoy more peaceful days.[6]

These words, I think, give us a clear portrait of the Roman Catholic veneration of Mary.

Parallels to others

You may have noticed that this encyclical made reference to Mary as "the second Eve." This is a popular parallel in Roman Catholic teaching. It mirrors the biblical parallel between Christ, the second Adam, and Adam himself. For instance, Paul writes: "Therefore, as through one man's offense judgment came to all men, resulting in condemnation, even so through one Man's righteous act the free gift came to all men, resulting in justification of life. For as by one man's disobedience many were made sinners, so also by one Man's obedience many will be made righteous" (Rom. 5:18–19).

Rome speaks of Mary as the second Eve, teaching that just as it was through one woman's disobedience that destruction came into the world, so it was through another woman's obedience that redemption came into the world. There is a parallel notion between the mother of destruction and the mother of redemption, the mother of sin and the mother of sanctity. This conjures up a representational role for Mary, the idea that Mary was not living and acting merely for herself alone but also for the human race, just as Eve did. As Pius XII put it in *Mystici Corporis Christi*, Mary "offered [Jesus] on Golgotha to the Eternal Father *for all the children of Adam*" (emphasis added). That was just the opposite of Eve offering the object of sin, the forbidden fruit, to her husband, although that act also represented something for all mankind.

Rome also teaches a parallel between Mary and Abraham. Just as Abraham was the father of the faithful (Rom. 4:11, 16), the Roman Catholic Church sees Mary as the mother of the faithful.

Mary also has been identified with the woman of Revelation 12. We read there:

And a great sign appeared in heaven: a woman clothed with the sun, with the moon under her feet, and on her head a crown of twelve stars. She was pregnant and was crying out in birth pains and the agony of giving birth. And another sign appeared in heaven: behold, a great red dragon, with seven heads and ten horns, and on his heads seven diadems. His tail swept down a third of the stars of heaven and cast them to the earth. And the dragon stood before the woman who was about to give birth, so that when she bore her child he might devour it. She gave birth to a male child, one who is to rule all the nations with a rod of iron, but her child was caught up to God and to his throne, and the woman fled into the wilderness, where she has a place prepared by God, in which she is to be nourished for 1,260 days. (Vv. 1–6)

In his Apostolic constitution, *Munificentissimus Deus*, Pius XII linked Mary with this unidentified woman, stating: "Moreover, the scholastic Doctors have recognized the Assumption of the Virgin Mother of God as something signified, not only in various figures of the Old Testament, but also in that woman clothed with the sun whom John the Apostle contemplated on the Island of Patmos."[7] That statement caused quite a bit of controversy among Roman Catholic biblical scholars, many of whom chastised the pope for this teaching. Nevertheless, it stands as an official statement regarding Mary.

Mary's fiat

Another Roman Catholic idea about Mary that is mentioned in *Mystici Corporis Christi* is the significance of Mary's fiat. In Luke 1, we find the record of the angel Gabriel's annunciation to Mary of the events that were about to transpire. We read there:

In the sixth month the angel Gabriel was sent from God to a city of Galilee named Nazareth, to a virgin betrothed to a man whose name was Joseph, of the house of David. And the virgin's name was Mary. And he came to her and said,

"Greetings, O favored one, the Lord is with you!" But she was greatly troubled at the saying, and tried to discern what sort of greeting this might be. And the angel said to her, "Do not be afraid, Mary, for you have found favor with God. And behold, you will conceive in your womb and bear a son, and you shall call his name Jesus. He will be great and will be called the Son of the Most High. And the Lord God will give to him the throne of his father David, and he will reign over the house of Jacob forever, and of his kingdom there will be no end." And Mary said to the angel, "How will this be, since I am a virgin?" And the angel answered her, "The Holy Spirit will come upon you, and the power of the Most High will overshadow you; therefore the child to be born will be called holy—the Son of God. And behold, your relative Elizabeth in her old age has also conceived a son, and this is the sixth month with her who was called barren. For nothing will be impossible with God." And Mary said, "Behold, I am the servant of the Lord; let it be to me according to your word." And the angel departed from her. (Vv. 26–38)

This passage records what Rome calls Mary's fiat, which, at least in some quarters of the Roman Catholic Church, is the most important biblical argument in favor of the notion that Mary is a Co-Redemptrix. What is this fiat? It is Mary's statement upon hearing the Lord's plan for her: "Behold, I am the servant of the Lord; let it be to me according to your word."

Historically, Protestants have interpreted that verse to mean that Mary willingly submitted to the announcement of God. The angel came and declared God's plans for Mary to bear the Savior. He stated what God was pleased to do. So, Mary acquiesced humbly and obediently, just as any child of God should acquiesce to His will. This was an act of supreme humility. She was saying, "If this is what the Lord wants, I am willing to do it." In the Protestant view, Mary was simply consenting to the Lord's will for her. Protestants see nothing in the announcement to indicate that the angel was asking for her permission.

According to Rome, however, Mary's statement was far more—it was a command. When Mary said "let it be," the Latin word used there is *fiat*, which is the imperative sense of the verb "to be." According to this view, Mary was saying, "Let it be so." She was making the command, and if she had not, then, at least according to the so-called maximalist position within the Roman Catholic Church, there would be no redemption. The whole act of redemption in Jesus Christ, the very incarnation itself, hung on Mary's response. Protestants might admit that God would never have violated Mary, that she could have said no theoretically. But her refusal certainly would not have shattered all hope for the redemption of God's people. However, from the Roman Catholic perspective, Mary *had* to be the one to bear the Savior. Why? Because she was the only sinless woman in the world.

Maximalists and minimalists

In contemporary Roman Catholicism, there is a debate between two Mariological parties, the maximalists and the minimalists. The difference is simple. The maximalists want to give maximum significance to Mary in the framework of redemption. The minimalists do not want to go so far.

The disagreement between these groups had a significant bearing on Vatican Council II, specifically, the adoption of the docket. Pope John XXIII said that the purpose of Vatican II was not to define doctrine, but there were some who wanted clarification as to where the church stood officially with regard to Mary in light of all the statements that had been made in the nineteenth and twentieth centuries.

Rufino Cardinal Santos, the archbishop of Manila, the Philippines, who represented the conservative wing of the church, called on the council to treat questions about Mary under the category of theology. Franz Cardinal König, the archbishop of Vienna, representing the more progressive Western wing, gave a speech advocating that Mary be discussed under ecclesiology rather than theology. In other words, König saw Mary as part of the notion of the church and not as a separate niche in the subdivision of our understanding of the things of God, of theology, a very significant difference. König's proposal was narrowly adopted. Remember, however, the pope had already declared that he did not want the council to deal with theological matters, so it is possible that some maximalists voted with the minimalists on this question out of deference to the pope's request. Even so, nearly half of the representation at Vatican II wanted to deal with Mary as a theological matter rather than as an ecclesiastical matter.

There are many differences between the maximalists and the minimalists, but the most basic difference is this: The maximalists want to emphasize that Mary's cooperation in our redemption by means of her fiat and her offering of the Son were utterly necessary to the incarnation and redemption. They take the position that without Mary's fiat, there would be no redemption. So, in the sense that redemption is completely and absolutely dependent on Mary's fiat, she could be called the Co-Redemptrix, and that would give further definition to the earlier papal statements about Mary's role in redeeming God's people. The minimalists, by contrast, want to view Mary not as Co-Redemptrix but as the supreme ecclesiastical type or exemplar of belief, the supreme model of Christian faith.

There is no objection from Protestants that Mary can be seen as one of the best, if not the best, models of belief. Years ago, I was invited to preach in a church on Mother's Day, and I preached on Mary. Afterward, many of the people told me they had never heard a sermon on Mary as the mother of Christ. They recounted Mother's Day sermons on Augustine's mother, Martin Luther's mother, John Calvin's mother, and so on, everyone, it seemed, but the mother of Jesus. We Protestants seem so eager to distance ourselves from Rome's position that we miss a magnificent example of godliness. I would venture to say that there is no better example of godliness in all of Scripture than Mary. I do not want her banished from the heritage of Protestantism; she is as much ours as anyone else's.

However, a Protestant willingness to see Mary as a model of faithfulness should not be confused with the Roman Catholic minimalist position. Those who hold the minimalist position affirm the doctrines of the immaculate conception, the bodily assumption, and the coronation. So, even the minimalist position is miles apart from the Protestant view.

Mariology or Mariolotry?

The basic question is whether the Roman Catholic preoccupation with Mary—the veneration of Mary, devotion to Mary, and so forth—adds up to Mariology or Mariolotry. To worship a human being, no matter how exemplary, faithful, and righteous he or she may be, is to engage in idolatry. Officially, the Roman Catholic Church does not sanction worship of Mary—but it comes very close. Rome sees a difference between what it calls *latria* and *dulia*. *Latria* is the Greek word for worship, while *dulia* is the Greek word for service. Giving *latria* to something other than God would be to worship an idol. Giving *dulia* is simply to give service, obeisance, or veneration, which can be given to things other than God. Rome made this same distinction with regard to statues during the iconoclastic controversy in the Reformation era; it said that when people bowed down and prayed before images, they were not worshiping them, they were merely doing service, using them as means to stimulate their own worship. Rome insists that Mary is given *dulia*, not *latria*; she is venerated but not worshiped.

However, for all practical purposes, I believe I can say without fear of ever being proven wrong that millions of Roman Catholic people today worship Mary. In doing so, they believe they are doing what the church is calling them to do. I grant that there is a legitimate technical distinction between *latria* and *dulia*, between worship and veneration, but it can be very hard to spot the line of separation. When people are bowing down before statues, that is of the essence of worship.

The biggest issue in the whole Mariology debate is the sufficiency of Christ. In truth, this is the issue with Roman Catholic theology from beginning to end. It is the issue with Rome's doctrine of Scripture, its doctrine of justification, and even here, with its doctrine of Mary. Is Christ alone our perfect sacrifice? Does He offer Himself for the sins of His people or is He offered by His mother? Does He alone achieve our redemption or does He have to depend upon the cooperation of His mother? Protestants believe that Christ alone is our justification. The Bible knows nothing of a parallel between Eve and Mary. It puts the emphasis on the parallel between Adam and Christ, who alone was the perfect sacrifice to undo what Adam caused once and for all.

Finally, there is the eschatological issue. The doctrine of the bodily assumption of Mary holds that God, in His grace, took Mary to heaven, where she now participates in all of the benefits that Christ has promised His people. Rome has said that this doctrine assures us of our participation in the resurrection of Christ. But the New Testament roots and grounds our assurance in Jesus' resurrection. We do not need another example; we simply need to believe the promises of Christ. By making this claim, Rome is adding to the New Testament witness that is the basis of our assurance of salvation and final redemption in Christ. This is an invention of men, not a result of the exegesis of the Word of God.

Roman Catholic and Protestant affirmations

The Catechism of the Catholic Church (1995) has much to say about Mary. Here are a few affirmations that touch on issues we have discussed, revealing that Rome continues to stand by these unbiblical positions:

> Through the centuries the Church has become ever more aware that Mary, "full of grace" through God, was redeemed from the moment of her conception. That is what the dogma of the Immaculate Conception confesses. (Section 491)

> "The Virgin Mary . . . is acknowledged and honored as being truly the Mother of God and of the redeemer. . . . She is 'clearly the mother of the members of Christ' . . . since she has by her charity joined in bringing about the birth of believers in the Church, who are members of its head." (963)

> "Finally the Immaculate Virgin, preserved free from all stain of original sin, when the course of her earthly life was finished, was taken up body and soul into heavenly glory, and exalted by the Lord as Queen over all things, so that she might be the more fully conformed to her Son, the Lord of lords and conqueror of sin and death" The Assumption of the Blessed Virgin is a singular participation in her Son's Resurrection and an anticipation of the resurrection of other Christians. (966)

> By her complete adherence to the Father's will, to his Son's redemptive work, and to every prompting of the Holy Spirit,

the Virgin Mary is the Church's model of faith and charity. Thus she is a "preeminent and . . . wholly unique member of the Church"; indeed, she is the "exemplary realization" of the church. (967)

"This motherhood of Mary in the order of grace continues uninterruptedly from the consent which she loyally gave at the Annunciation and which she sustained without wavering beneath the cross, until the eternal fulfillment of all the elect. Taken up to heaven she did not lay aside this saving office but by her manifold intercession continues to bring us the gifts of eternal salvation. . . . Therefore the Blessed Virginia is invoked in the Church under the titles of Advocate, Helper, Benefactress, and Mediatrix. (969)

"The Church's devotion to the Blessed Virgin is intrinsic to Christian worship." The Church rightly honors "the Blessed Virgin with special devotion. From the most ancient times the Blessed Virgin has been honored with the title of 'Mother of God,' to whose protection the faithful fly in all their dangers and needs. . . . This very special devotion . . . differs essentially from the adoration which is given to the incarnate Word and equally to the Father and the Holy Spirit, and greatly fosters this adoration." The liturgical feasts dedicated to the Mother of God and Marian prayer, such as the rosary, an "epitome of the whole Gospel," express this devotion to the Virgin Mary. (971)

By pronouncing her "fiat" at the Annunciation and giving her consent to the Incarnation, Mary was already collaborating with the whole work her Son was to accomplish. She is mother wherever he is Savior and head of the Mystical Body. (973)

The Most Blessed Virgin Mary, when the course of her earthly life was completed, was taken up body and soul into the glory of heaven, where she already shares in the glory of her Son's Resurrection, anticipating the resurrection of all members of His Body. (974)

"We believe that the Holy Mother of God, the new Eve, Mother of the Church, continues in heaven to exercise her maternal role on behalf of the members of Christ." (975)

The Protestant Reformers had little to say about Mary. If they failed to give her her due as an example of godliness, it was no doubt because of their zeal to avoid the excesses of Rome. The Westminster Confession of Faith makes only one mention of Mary, maintaining an eloquent silence in opposition to all the roles she is accorded in Roman Catholic theology:

The Son of God, the second Person in the Trinity, being very and eternal God, of one substance, and equal with the Father, did, when the fullness of time was come, take upon him man's nature, with all the essential properties and common infirmities thereof; yet without sin: being conceived by the power of the Holy Ghost, in the womb of the Virgin Mary, of her substance. So that two whole, perfect, and distinct natures, the Godhead and the manhood, were inseparably joined together in one person, without conversion, composition, or confusion. Which person is very God and very man, yet one Christ, the only Mediator between God and man. (8.2)

The Roman Catholic attitude toward Mary represents much that is problematic with Rome's approach to the Christian faith.

Its teachings about Mary go far beyond scriptural warrant and represent the ideas of men. Furthermore, they strike at the very basis of Protestant belief about salvation—justification by Christ alone. Protestants must continue to stand firm on *solus Christus*.

HOW THEN SHOULD WE PROCEED?

I HAVE WRITTEN IN STRONG terms in this book because I believe the errors of the Roman Catholic Church are deep and significant. As I noted in the introduction, I am happy to make common cause with Roman Catholics on social issues, but we have no common cause in the gospel. Rome has compromised the gospel with her unbiblical doctrines. I firmly believe that she is "teaching as doctrines the commandments of men" (Matt. 15:9).

How then should we proceed? How should we relate to Roman Catholics?

I believe that as individuals, we should reach out to Roman Catholics. We should love our neighbors who are in the Church of Rome. We should befriend them and spend time with them. By doing so, we earn the right to lovingly critique their views.

As churches, we must stand for the biblical gospel—and nothing more. It is our calling to hold high the truth and expose falsehood. To this end, it is essential that we know and understand what Rome is teaching, so distinctions can be made. It is important that the people in the pews be educated about what Protestants believe over against what Roman Catholics teach.

Pastors should preach the gospel and point out ways in which it is twisted by men, including the Roman Catholic Church. I am not saying that every sermon must attack Rome, but given the attraction that Roman Catholicism is exerting on some Protestants, it is essential that its errors be exposed. By faithfully preaching the gospel, pastors will defend the Reformation.

When our involvement in social issues brings us into contact and camaraderie with Roman Catholics, we need not draw back. But we must not assume that we are brothers and sisters with them in the gospel. They are members of a church that has anathematized the gospel, so we ought to pray for them and seek to reach them for Christ.

There is much more I could have said in this book, many other topics of Roman Catholic belief and practice I could have dissected. However, I hope this small book has introduced you to some of the issues that have been—and remain—in dispute between Protestants and Roman Catholics. I encourage you to dig deeper on your own so that you will become more knowledgeable and articulate in dealing with these issues. Much is at stake, and there is a desperate need for an educated laity.

The Reformation is not over. It cannot be over and must not be over until all who call themselves Christians have one Lord, one faith, and one baptism. The cause of *sola Scriptura, sola fide, sola gratia, solus Christus*, and *soli Deo Gloria* remains the cause of and for biblical truth.

NOTES

Introduction

1 "As regards those who, by sin, have fallen from the received grace of Justification, they may be again justified, when, God exciting them, through the sacrament of Penance they shall have attained to the recovery, by the merit of Christ, of the grace lost: for this manner of Justification is of the fallen the reparation: which the holy Fathers have aptly called a second plank after the shipwreck of grace lost." (Canons and Decrees of the Council of Trent, Sixth Session, Chap. XIV, http://history.hanover.edu/texts/trent/trentall.html, accessed March 12, 2012.)

2 "If any one saith, that by faith alone the impious is justified; in such wise as to mean, that nothing else is required to co-operate in order to the obtaining the grace of Justification, and that it is not in any way necessary, that he be prepared and disposed by the movement of his own will; let him be anathema." (Canons and Decrees of the Council of Trent, Sixth Session, Chap. XVI, Canon IX, http://history.hanover.edu/texts/trent/trentall.html, accessed March 12, 2012.)

3 Evangelicals & Catholics Together: The Christian Mission in the Third Millennium, http://www.leaderu.com/ftissues/ft9405/articles/mission .html, accessed March 12, 2012.

4 The Manhattan Declaration: A Call of Christian Conscience, http:// manhattandeclaration.org/the-declaration/read.aspx, accessed March 12, 2012.

5 G. C. Berkouwer, *Vatikaans Concilie en Nieuwe Theologie* (Kampen: JH Kok N.V., 1964), 15.

6 Mark A. Noll and Carolyn Nystrom, *Is the Reformation Over? An Evangelical Assessment of Contemporary Roman Catholicism* (Grand Rapids: Baker Academic, 2005). "Things Are Not the Way They Used to Be" is the title of chapter 1.

7 From the hymn "A Mighty Fortress Is Our God" by Martin Luther, 1529.

Chapter One

1 Martin Luther, cited in Roland H. Bainton, *Here I Stand: A Life of Martin Luther* (Nashville: Abingdon Press, 1950), 144. Bainton notes that the words "Here I stand. I cannot do otherwise" are not in the earliest printed versions, but that may have been because the listeners were too moved to take notes at that point.

2 Canons and Decrees of the Council of Trent, Fourth Session, http://history.hanover .edu/texts/trent/trentall.html, accessed March 13, 2012.

3 Vatican Ecumenical Council I Decrees, Session 3: 24 April 1870—Dogmatic Constitution on the Catholic Faith, chapter 2, http://www.intratext.com/IXT /ENG0063/_P6.HTM, accessed March 13, 2012.

4 Ibid.

5 Hans Küng, *Infallible? An Inquiry*, trans. Edward Quinn (Garden City, N.Y.: Doubleday, 1971), 174.

6 *Divino Afflante Spiritu*, http://www.papalencyclicals.net/Pius12/P12DIVIN.HTM, accessed March 13, 2012.

7 Ibid.

8 Ibid.

9 Ibid.

10 Ibid.

11 Vatican Ecumenical Council II Documents, *Dei Verbum*, Dogmatic Constitution on Divine Revelation, Chap. 3, http://www.intratext.com/IXT/ENG0037/_P4.HTM, accessed March 13, 2012.

12 Canons and Decrees of the Council of Trent, Fourth Session, http://history.hanover .edu/texts/trent/trentall.html, accessed March 13, 2012.

13 G. C. Berkouwer, *Vatikaans Concilie en Nieuwe Theologie* (Kampen: JH Kok N.V., 1964), 111–13.

14 All citations of the Roman Catholic catechism are from *Catechism of the Catholic Church*, Second Edition (New York: Doubleday, 1995).

15 Canons and Decrees of the Council of Trent, Fourth Session, http://history.hanover .edu/texts/trent/trentall.html, accessed March 13, 2012.

Chapter Two

1 Canons and Decrees of the Council of Trent, Sixth Session, Chap. V, http://history.hanover.edu/texts/trent/trentall.html, accessed March 14, 2012.

2 John Calvin, *Institutes of the Christian Religion*, ed. John T. McNeill, trans. Ford Lewis Battles, The Library of Christian Classics, Vols. 20–21 (Philadelphia: The Westminster Press, 1960), 2.8.59; 3.4.28.

3 Canons and Decrees of the Council of Trent, Sixth Session, Chap. XIV, http://history.hanover.edu/texts/trent/trentall.html, accessed March 14, 2012.

Chapter Three

1 Ecumenical Council of Florence, Session 11, http://www.ewtn.com/library/ COUNCILS/FLORENCE.HTM, accessed March 15, 2012. This sentiment was echoed in certain statements made by Vatican Council I.

2 *Quanto Conficiamur Moerore*, Section 7, http://www.papalencyclicals.net/Pius09/ p9quanto.htm, accessed March 15, 2012.

3 Ibid., Section 8.

4 *Presbyterorum Ordinis*, Chap. 1, http://www.vatican.va/archive/hist_councils/ ii_vatican_council/documents/vat-ii_decree_19651207_presbyterorum-ordinis_ en.html, accessed March 15, 2012.

5 Responses to Some Questions Regarding Certain Aspects of the Doctrine on the Church, Fifth Question, http://www.doctrinafidei.va/documents/rc_con_cfaith_ doc_20070629_responsa-quaestiones_en.html, accessed March 15, 2012.

Chapter Four

1 Canons and Decrees of the Council of Trent, Sixth Session, Chap. XIV, http:// history.hanover.edu/texts/trent/trentall.html, accessed March 16, 2012.

2 *Mysterium Fidei*, http://www.papalencyclicals.net/Paul06/p6myster.htm, accessed March 16, 2012.

Chapter Five

1 Syllabus of Errors, #18, http://www.ewtn.com/library/PAPALDOC/P9SYLL.HTM, accessed March 19, 2012.

2 Hans Küng, *Infallible? An Inquiry*, trans. Edward Quinn (Garden City, N.Y.: Doubleday, 1971), 92–93.

3 Vatican Ecumenical Council I Decrees, Session 4: 18 July 1870—First Dogmatic Constitution on the Church of Christ, http://www.intratext.com/IXT/ENG0063/_ PD.HTM, accessed March 19, 2012.

4 Canons and Decrees of the Council of Trent, Sixth Session, Chap. XVI, Canon IX, http://history.hanover.edu/texts/trent/trentall.html, accessed March 19, 2012.

5 Vatican Ecumenical Council I Decrees, Session 4: 18 July 1870—First Dogmatic Constitution on the Church of Christ, Chap. 1, http://www.intratext.com/IXT/ ENG0063/_PE.HTM, accessed March 19, 2012.

6 Ibid., Chap. 2.

7 Ibid., Chap. 3.

8 Ibid., Chap. 4.

9 Vatican Ecumenical Council II Documents, *Lumen Gentium*, Dogmatic Constitution on the Church, Chap. 3, http://www.intratext.com/IXT /ENG0037/_PA.HTM, accessed March 19, 2012.

10 Ibid.

11 Ibid.

Chapter Six

1 Jaroslav Pelikan, *Mary Through the Centuries* (New Haven, Conn.: Yale University Press, 1996), 55.

2 *Mystici Corporis Christi*, Section 110, http://www.papalencyclicals.net/Pius12 /P12MYSTI.HTM, accessed March 20, 2012.

3 Ibid.

4 Ibid.

5 Ibid.

6 Ibid., Section 111.

7 *Munificentissimus Deus*, section 27, http://www.papalencyclicals.net/Pius12 /P12MUNIF.HTM, accessed March 20, 2012.

INDEX

ABOUT THE AUTHOR

Dr. R. C. Sproul is the founder and chairman of Ligonier Ministries, an international Christian education ministry based near Orlando, Florida. He also serves as copastor of Saint Andrew's Chapel in Sanford, Florida, and as the chancellor of Reformation Bible College. His teaching can be heard on the daily radio program *Renewing Your Mind*.

During his distinguished academic career, Dr. Sproul helped train men for the ministry as a professor at several theological seminaries.

He is the author of more than one hundred books, including *The Holiness of God, Chosen by God, The Invisible Hand, Faith Alone, A Taste of Heaven, Truths We Confess, The Truth of the Cross*, and *The Prayer of the Lord*. He also served as general editor of the *Reformation Study Bible* and has written several children's books, including *The Knight's Map*.

Dr. Sproul and his wife, Vesta, make their home in Sanford, Florida.